NEW STUDIES IN BIBLICAL THEOLOGY

D. A. Carson, Series Editor

NEW STUDIES IN BIBLICAL THEOLOGY

Possessed by God
DAVID PETERSON

Whoredom
RAYMOND C. ORTLUND, JR.

Jesus and the Logic of History
PAUL W. BARNETT

Hear, My Son
DANIEL J. ESTES

Original Sin
HENRI BLOCHER

Original Sin

ILLUMINATING THE RIDDLE

Henri Blocher

WILLIAM B. EERDMANS PUBLISHING COMPANY
GRAND RAPIDS, MICHIGAN / CAMBRIDGE, U.K.

© 1997 Henri Blocher

First published 1997 in the U.K. by
APOLLOS (an imprint of Inter-Varsity Press)

This edition published 1999 in the United States of America by
Wm. B. Eerdmans Publishing Co.
255 Jefferson Ave. S.E., Grand Rapids, Michigan 49503 /
P.O. Box 163, Cambridge CB3 9PU U.K.

Printed in the United States of America

04 03 02 01 00 99   7 6 5 4 3 2 1

Library of Congress Cataloging-in-Publication Data

Blocher, Henri.
Original sin : Illuminating the riddle / by Henri Blocher.
p.   cm. – (New studies in biblical theology)
Includes bibliographical references and indexes.
ISBN 8028-4411-1 (pbk. : alk. paper)
1. Sin, Original – Biblical teaching. I. Title. II. Series.
BT720.B565   1999
233'.14 – dc21   98-53406
CIP

Contents

Series preface

New Studies in Biblical Theology is a series of monographs that address key issues in the discipline of biblical theology. Contributions to the series focus on one or more of three areas: 1. the nature and status of biblical theology, including its relations with other disciplines (*e.g.* historical theology, exegesis, systematic theology, historical criticism, narrative theology); 2. the articulation and exposition of the structure of thought of a particular biblical writer or corpus; and 3. the delineation of a biblical theme across all or part of the biblical corpora.

Above all, these monographs are creative attempts to help thinking Christians understand their Bibles better. The series aims simultaneously to instruct and to edify, to interact with the current literature, and to point the way ahead. In God's universe, mind and heart should not be divorced: in this series we will try not to separate what God has joined together. While the notes interact with the best of the scholarly literature, the text is uncluttered with untransliterated Greek and Hebrew, and tries to avoid too much technical jargon. The volumes are written within the framework of confessional evangelicalism, but there is always an attempt at thoughtful engagement with the sweep of the relevant literature.

Henri Blocher is a theologian of the very first rank, and still too little known outside the francophone world. Steeped in the Reformed tradition, he is not chained by it, as this volume attests; he is able to think through the interlocking contributions of historical theology, biblical theology and systematic theology, and come to fresh conclusions in the light of Scripture, without overturning all that is valuable from the past. But this book has an importance beyond its contribution to reflection on original sin. Western culture has moved away from thinking that the human dilemma is bound up with sin that calls for repentance; it prefers to think that our dilemma is bound up with epistemology that calls for creative discourse that remakes our world. We no longer answer to the God who is our Maker and Judge; we answer to our restrictive interpretative communities. In such a world, it is important for Christians to think systemically about their faith, for we are involved in a systemic worldview clash whose parameters become more sharply focused with every passing year. If we cannot agree on what the problem is, we certainly cannot agree on what the solution is – which in this case jeopardizes the gospel itself. So this is a book to be read and thought through with great care.

D. A. Carson
Trinity Evangelical Divinity School,
Deerfield, Illinois

Preface

The chapters which comprise this book are based upon the annual Moore College Lectures delivered in Sydney, Australia, in August 1995. I wish to express first and foremost my deep gratitude for the invitation that was extended to me (a distinct honour and pleasure), and to say how delightful a memory I have of the wonderful hospitality extended by the Principal, Dr Peter Jensen, and his wife; the whole faculty; and the student body. I shall not forget the Australian warmth and the enriching exchanges that I enjoyed at Moore College.

I am also most grateful to Professor D. A. Carson, the Series Editor, for his valuable comments and friendly patience; similarly to the Rev. David Kingdon, the former Theological Books Editor of Inter-Varsity Press, and to his successor Dr Mark D. J. Smith; and to my son Jacques, who read through the manuscript at various stages and gave me sorely needed computer help. I should add my many thanks to the librarians of Moore College, of the Faculté Libre de Théologie Evangélique at Vaux-sur-Seine, France, and of the Faculté de Théologie Evangélique at Montreal, Quebec: they fuelled the engine, and without their assistance it would not have moved very far.

Only very common abbreviations have been used; they require no explanation. Unless otherwise indicated, I have made my own translation when quoting the words of Scripture; quotations marked 'NIV' are taken from the New International Version (1973, 1978, 1984), and those marked 'NEB' from the New English Bible (1961–1970).

Henri Blocher

Introduction

'The Devil is wildly optimistic if he thinks he can make human beings worse than they are.' One could hardly conceive of a darker flash of wit than this judgment from an acute observer of a former generation, the Viennese writer Karl Kraus (1874–1936).

Kraus's satirical barb surely earns him a front-row seat among pessimists, but who can deny that it touches reality? It certainly holds at least a measure of realism at the end of the century of Auschwitz and Kigali, of Beirut and Bosnia, of the Gulag Archipelago and daily terror in Algeria. Could we sink any lower in mass cruelty and wickedness? In addition, 'private' horrors seem to match the socio-political atrocities: the rising tide of divorce and abortion, the abuse and prostitution of children, corruption in business; the constant praise of immorality by the brightest luminaries of our culture, and a taste for lying; sheer despair on all hands; millions of young people apparently without a future.

The phenomenon of human evil, so widespread, so pervasive, cries out for an explanation, or at least for an examination. Dumbfounded grief should not be our final reaction, for a threefold question arises.

First, why is the perception of human evil, in the main, accompanied by feelings of indignation, guilt or shame? If human evil were merely 'natural', like the ferocity of tigers (or ants!), there would be no room for such feelings. Bound up with our sure sense of human evil, we find the conviction that it occurs through the exercise of some kind of 'freedom'.

Secondly, if humans are capable of so much evil, how is it that they also reach heights of heroism, performing admirable deeds of selfless service and devotion to the truth? How can they bear fruits of beauty and wisdom? The brighter side, which Karl Kraus seemed to ignore, should keep us from cynicism; we have to acknowledge the complexity of the human phenomenon.

But how can we account for that complexity? What insight or revelation will provide an Ariadne's thread to save us from being

11

lost in the labyrinth? Actually, the complexity is worse than many imagine; one may discover worthy motives in outrageous actions, and ugly roots under the flowering of virtue. How can we make sense of the entanglement of these things?

Thirdly, for those who have discerned that the world is not self-explanatory, but that it owes its origin to a holy and wise Creator, the presence and power of evil in human life make the need for a word of assurance and clarification even more urgent. Without it, how can we face the apparent contradiction?

The Christian doctrine of original sin is designed to deal with this threefold question. It tries to account for sin as a universal phenomenon and yet a matter of personal responsibility, for its being 'natural' in a sense and yet contrary to our true 'nature', for its being there even as we stand before God and under God. Cardinal Newman (1893: 242f.) forcefully expressed the need for the doctrine if we are not to ignore the 'success' of evil in our world while knowing our God:

> . . . either there is no Creator, or this living society of
> men is in a true sense discarded from His presence . . .
> And so I argue about the world; – *if* there be a God, *since*
> there is a God, the human race is implicated in some
> terrible aboriginal calamity. It is out of joint with the
> purposes of its Creator. This is a fact, a fact as true as the
> fact of its existence; and thus the doctrine of what is
> theologically called original sin becomes to me almost
> as certain as that the world exists, and as the existence of
> God.

If the doctrine or dogma of original sin has always been an essential part of a Christian assessment of reality, the traumas of our time heighten its relevance. Nevertheless, it has been somewhat neglected in recent decades. The reason may be that it is hard to fit within the framework of 'modernity', of modern (and postmodern) presuppositions – not to say prejudices. As prestigious a philosopher as Leszek Kolakowski (formerly a Marxist) has had to warn theologians not to put the light of the doctrine of original sin under a bushel.[1]

[1] As we are reminded by Schönborn 1991a: 10. Schönborn (now Archbishop of Vienna) denounces the paradox of the modern sense of evil; it is acute in many respects, and yet it denies original sin.

In this book, we shall heed the admonition, and gather as much light as we are able to find in the pages of Holy Scripture, our only Norm (*norma normans*), the divine instruction of the Lord's people. This enquiry, which impinges on the subject area of my earlier publications *In the Beginning* (1984) and *Evil and the Cross* (1994), draws on the work of many predecessors, among whom readers will notice the frequently recurring names of Augustine, François Turretin, Blaise Pascal, Jonathan Edwards, Søren Kierkegaard, John Murray and Paul Ricœur, to whom I am indebted in various regards. We treasure tradition not by servile adherence to it, but by, as it were, sitting on the shoulders of fathers and elder brothers who were giants indeed, and thus do we hope to be granted the grace of seeing even further and ever more clearly.

Chapter One

Original sin as taught in Holy Scripture

'Nothing is so easy to denounce, nothing is so difficult to understand.' So wrote Augustine on original sin.[1]

To him the doctrine was a battlefield. The controversy has continued unabated through the centuries. The leaders of the Reformation, with the exception of Ulrich Zwingli,[2] renewed the emphasis on the Augustinian view. It was included in the main confessions of faith in the Reformation churches, such as the Forty-two Articles framed by Archbishop Cranmer for the Church of England in 1553. The arguments have not subsided; Protestant liberals carry on the various attacks against the doctrine of original sin which the Socinians and some Anabaptists had launched in the sixteenth century. The perpetual conflict probably witnesses both to the difficulty of the arguments and to the stakes involved.

A new stage was reached (and new heights in subtlety and sophistication) in the first half of the twentieth century with the powerful neo-orthodox reinterpretation of the doctrine. In the wake of Kierkegaard's elusive *The Concept of Anxiety* (1844), Karl Barth, Emil Brunner and Reinhold Niebuhr – who praised Kierkegaard's analysis as 'the profoundest in Christian thought' (Niebuhr 1941: 182 n. 2) – again preached original sin, but not without making far-reaching changes in their understanding of it.

---

[1] 'Nihil est ad praedicandum notius, nihil ad intelligendum secretius' (the first part could also be rendered, 'No fact is better known, or established, for one to comment upon'): *De moribus catholicae ecclesiae* XXII.40. Augustine is referring to the 'ancient sin', *antiquum peccatum*. In the same paragraph, he deals with the soul's 'heavy chain', the body, as a consequence of sin.

[2] Zwingli had expressed a preference for the word *Erbprest*, 'original weakness, or sickness' over against the traditional word *Erbsünd*, 'original sin'. But *Erbprest* gave insufficient grounds for condemnation. The learned Anabaptist leader Balthasar Hubmaier took him to task on this issue, and made a strong Augustinian stand. Zwingli was compelled to refine his position. See Pipkin and Yoder 1989: 285 with n. 41.

Among evangelical theologians, John Murray's series of short, sharp articles, published under the title *The Imputation of Adam's Sin* (1959) and G. C. Berkouwer's *Sin* (first Dutch edition 1959–60) illustrate two contrasting kinds of original thinking within orthodox bounds: the former with rigour and careful argument; the latter with well-informed sensitivity and openness to the concerns of contemporary theology – but still confessing, in a softer, more sympathetically nuanced tone, the main tenets of Reformed tradition. Both contributions still deserve our full consideration.

Has controversy cooled since then? After years of comparative neglect, at least in Protestant circles, there are signs that interest in the doctrine may be awakening. Feminist process theologian Marjorie Hewitt Suchocki has set out a vigorous reply to Niebuhr on original sin (Suchocki 1994). The American Lutheran professor Ted Peters does theology in a lively, thought-provoking way, raising deep questions on the subject of original sin (Peters 1994). Professor David L. Smith in Canada (though an heir to the US Southern Baptist tradition) has produced a most user-friendly presentation (Smith 1994), which follows in the train of Bernard Ramm's moderate synthesis of evangelical substance and modern ideas a decade earlier (Ramm 1985) – the first token, maybe, of attention being paid to the old doctrine again. The contributions of these competent scholars are not great in number; they are, rather, wide-ranging, and semi-popular in style. They leave enough room, therefore, for a more concentrated study, one which may also take more notice of the work of Roman Catholic theologians from continental Europe.

There is no urgent need to rehearse the history of the doctrine. It has been covered in a number of monographs, and Norman P. Williams's classic (1927), though sorely lacking in sympathy for Augustine, offers sufficient resources.[3] My aim, as my sub-title suggests, will rather be to *illuminate the riddle.* Original sin is a riddle, certainly, and I dare hope that this book will cast some light upon it (*audentes fortuna juvat!*); even more importantly, however, the *human phenomenon* is a riddle, and I

---

[3] Smith 1994 summarizes later developments. In French, there is Rondet 1967, and in German, the massive work (four volumes) is that of Gross 1960–72.

trust that the doctrine of original sin will illuminate that phenomenon.

This book will be an exercise in dogmatics, not apologetics – in this, I agree with Kierkegaard, who insisted that original sin comes under the jurisdiction of dogmatics (1980: sub-titles 9, 23 and *passim*). There may be some incidental apologetic benefits, but the central question will be: what are we to believe, in the obedience of faith? Since the first concern of evangelical dogmatics, in grateful obedience to its 'external principle of knowledge', is agreement with Scripture, I shall enquire first (chapter 1) about the general support which may be found in the whole Bible for the church dogma, that is, the 'Augustinian' doctrine, of original sin. I shall be wary of the enticements of those who follow Karl Barth's lead[4] and draw their theology of sin from Christ and the cross *directly*. Though apparently most 'Christian', this procedure conceals a subtle snare: the selection and abstraction of the relevant elements of Christology, a complex field of study, is bound to be arbitrary. If one starts with the cross, the character of Christ's work as a remedy for sin, as redemption, is obscured;[5] simply to read the meaning of original sin off the Christ-event is to act as if we were masters of revelation. Far from it! We are mere disciples, and cannot afford not to start with the teaching of God. Sound theological method requires that we listen to Scripture as a whole, according to the analogy of faith, and only then perceive how precisely the doctrine is proclaimed and, so to speak, reinforced in the Christ-event.

The path to be travelled by this volume is fairly easy to mark out. Once the biblical survey is completed, we shall turn to *the*

---

[4] Barth (1957: 739) could write of Jesus Christ: 'He is the man whom God in His eternal counsel, giving Him the command, treated as its transgressor, thus rejecting Him in His righteous wrath, and actually threatening Him with that final dereliction. That this was true of Adam, and is true of us, is the case only because in God's counsel, and in the event of Golgotha, it became true first of all in Jesus Christ.' Barth's 'first of all' powerfully expresses his bold and decisive reversal of the Adam–Christ order. (*Cf.* the same reversal for Adam's innocence, p. 740.)

[5] Pannenberg (1994: 252 n. 258) also criticizes Barth's method: 'he did not see that uncovering sin in the light of the revelation in Christ relates to something that is more universal by nature and that precedes the revelation. Failure to see this means making the fact of sin a mere postulate of the Christian faith.'

'origin' passage, Genesis 3, asking whether we should read it as history or as myth, saga or symbol (chapter 2). Then the other scripture upon which the doctrine of original sin was founded, Romans 5, will engage our scrutiny (chapter 3); against all the odds, will a new proposal break through the deadlock of interpretations ancient and modern? In the next chapter (4), we shall observe how the doctrine of 'original sin' unveils human experience, unlocks the enigmas of life and sets them in proper perspective. Finally, we shall confront the core difficulty of Augustine's construction: the hereditary transmission of what is a most personal exercise of freedom, namely, sin.

First, though, we need some idea of just what it is we are talking about. Calvin's definition offers as good a starting-point as any. Original sin, he writes in the *Institutes*, is that 'hereditary depravity and corruption of our nature, diffused into all parts of the soul, which first makes us liable to God's wrath, then also brings forth in us those works which Scripture calls "works of the flesh" (Gal. 5:19)' (II.i.8). By way of developing and commenting on that definition, we may note the following four points. First, original sin is *universal sinfulness*, consisting of attitudes, orientations, propensities and tendencies which are contrary to God's law, incompatible with his holiness, and found in all people, in all areas of their lives. Secondly, it belongs to the *nature* of human beings (it is also called *peccatum naturale*), 'nature' being that stable complex of characteristics typical of the class of creatures known as 'human', and present from birth (*natura* comes from *nasci*, 'to be born'). Thirdly, since it belongs to our nature, it is *inherited*; hence its usual name in German, *Erbsünde*, literally 'hereditary sin'. Fourthly, it *stems from Adam*, whose disobedience gave original sin a historical beginning, so that the present sinfulness of all can be traced back through the generations, to the first man and progenitor of the race.

The 'origin' of original sin is touched on in John 8:44, which speaks of the *archē* of the devil's murderous lie. This is the 'enemy' whom Revelation calls the 'original (*archaios*) serpent (12:9; 20:2). Augustine preferred 'original' to 'natural' as a qualifying term in order to stipulate that universal sinfulness had a historical beginning and cause.[6] The famous Genevan

---

[6] As noticed by Vanneste (1994: 376), quoting in n. 82 the *Opus imperfectum contra Iulianum* V. 9.

theologian François Turretin, who won the title of the 'Protestant Aquinas', made the perceptive remark that sin is not radically original, since it derives not from the first origin (creation) but from a second one; yet, he maintained, the term is apt because original sin flows from the originating sin, propagates itself in each person's origination, and becomes the origin of actual sins (1847: 569 [IX.10.4]). 'Actual sins' are all other sins, though the demarcation line is hard to draw, as older divines recognized.[7] In Judaism, we are told, 'a distinction was drawn between the original stock or capital (so-called original sin; Heb. *qeren*) and interest (individual sins)' (Hensel 1975: 721). It is probably wise therefore to think of both in the closest possible organic conjunction.

Actual sins incur guilt. The traditional Augustinian line is that original sin does too, and Calvin's definition, 'liable to God's wrath', implies it clearly. But not all are so tough-minded. Many have doubted whether, in the Christian tradition, there is a concept of true original *guilt*. If we speak, as Cyprian did, of an alien sin,[8] is not the phrase 'alien guilt' a contradiction in terms?

The scandal seems even greater when *heredity* is the stated mode of transmission. Karl Barth vehemently rejects the idea, and with it the term *Erbsünde*. ' "Hereditary sin" has a hopelessly naturalistic, deterministic and even fatalistic ring. If both parts of the term are taken seriously, it is a *contradictio in adjecto* in face of which there is no help for it but to juggle away either the one part or the other' (1956: 501). Even those who hold to the traditional thesis still have to think *how* sin and guilt can be inherited.

To the law and the testimony! Does Scripture support, at least in broad terms, the doctrine I have just delineated?

Universal sinfulness

That a bent towards sinning does affect all humankind, and that

---

[7] Brunner (1947: 117 n. 1) quotes Johann Gerhard, *Loci theologici* V.17: 'Original sin and actual sins are so joined that it would be difficult to show a quibbler the mathematical point at which they may be distinguished' (my translation).

[8] Of infants, Cyprian says in his 64th Epistle, 'remittuntur non propria sed aliena peccata' ('not their own but alien sins are remitted'); quoted by Williams 1927: 295.

it cannot be isolated as belonging to any one part of the person, has been agreed on all sides, or nearly so, in the twentieth century. Even those who oppose the church dogma of original sin concur in this basic assessment of our reality. It would be hard to close one's eyes to the data of experience. The value of solidarity, highly prized in the modern scale of values, forbids one to draw radical distinctions between individuals,[9] and the renewed perception that the individual is a psychosomatic unity does not favour a division between 'parts' of the person with regard to sinfulness.

The witness of Scripture fully warrants this consensus. It majors on sinfulness as *the* human problem, which alone causes separation between the Creator and his creatures (Is. 59:2). It stresses that none escapes the reign of sin and that no part of the human person is left untainted (Pr. 20:9; Ps. 14; and Paul's quotations in Rom. 3:10ff.). But it does not formally distinguish our proneness to evil from our sinful acts or failures to act. Yet the twofold universal spread of actual sin (that is, throughout the whole race and within the whole individual life) could hardly obtain without an equally universal bent, or corruption. The Bible itself explicitly follows that logic.

Illustrations abound. As early as the case of Cain, sin is depicted as 'crouching at the door', implying an impulse or desire which Cain ought to master (Gn. 4:7).[10] For Paul also, sin, ever ready to cause all manner of evil, is 'lying there' (*parakeitai*, Rom. 7:21), a tyrant 'indwelling' his members (v. 17); a few verses earlier, sin resembles a snake, apparently lying dead within the person, which springs to life in the presence of the commandment (vv. 8–11). James's letter highlights the process that gives birth to particular sinful acts; the source is the person's own *epithymia*, 'concupiscence' or inordinate desire (Jas. 1:14). Ligier (1960: 106f.) interprets the 'stubbornness' of the heart, which Jeremiah so often denounces (3:17; 7:24; 9:14; 11:8; *etc.*), as a passionate impulse of freedom, an anarchic unloosing which cannot but issue in disobedience.[11] The same idea of the existence of sin before sins are committed is

---

[9] Pannenberg (1994: 238) speaks of the 'antimoralistic function' of the doctrine of original sin as it preserves solidarity with evildoers.

[10] The same (rare) word is used as in Gn. 3:16 for the woman's desire.

[11] He disagrees with the usual rendering 'stubbornness' for *šrîrût* (appealing to Joüon).

suggested by the metaphors of sin written upon the heart (Je. 17:1), of heart and ears uncircumcised (Je. 6:10, 9:25f.; cf. 4:4 and Dt. 10:16; 30:6; Acts 7:51) and of the heart being of stone (Ezk. 11:19). Our Lord himself stressed that all the things that truly defile people originate in their hearts (Mt. 15:19f. and par.), and that evil words flow from what fills their hearts, and evil deeds from what is stored up within (Mt. 12:34ff.).

In somewhat analogous fashion, Judaism developed the theme of the 'evil imagination' or 'impulse' in human make-up, yēṣer ra'. The phrase was taken from Genesis 6:5, 'every inclination [or impulse, or imagination, yēṣer] was only evil all the time'. Murray's comment on that passage is worth quoting:

> There is the *intensity* – 'The wickedness of man was great in the earth'; there is the *inwardness* – 'the imagination of the thoughts of his heart', an expression unsurpassed in the usage of Scripture to indicate that the most rudimentary movement of thought was evil; there is the *totality* – 'every imagination'; there is the *constancy* – 'continually'; there is the *exclusiveness* – 'only evil'; there is the *early manifestation* – 'from his youth' (1962: 1191f.).

The last trait comes from Genesis 8:21, a verse which shows that the truth of the statement in 6:5 is not restricted to the situation before the flood. Intertestamental literature elaborates the theme, sometimes with a *good* impulse in view too. As early as the book of Ecclesiasticus, the pathetic question is raised: 'O evil imagination [*enthymēma*], whence were you formed to cover the land with deceit?' (37:3). At the end of the first century AD, *4 Ezra* uses, in the extant Latin text, the words 'malignant heart' (*cor malignum*) as a probable equivalent: 'The First Adam, bearing the malignant heart, trespassed and was defeated, and [so were] all those who are born of him; this weakness [*infirmitas*] has become permanent . . .' (3:21f.); 'the malignant heart has grown within us; it has turned us away from [your] commandments, and led us into corruption and on the ways of death . . .' (7:48). The theme may also be found in the Qumran hymns:

> No-one will be justified in your judgment.
> Nor be shown innocent in your trial.

A human being proceeding from a human being, can
    he be righteous?
A man coming from a man, can he deal wisely?
And flesh coming from the *evil inclination,* can it share
    in glory?

(*1 QH* IX.14d–16)[12]

In several New Testament passages, the presence of the *yēṣer*
may be detected as the underlying theme. It may be the original
word behind the 'evil thoughts' of Matthew 15:19;[13] it may be
represented by 'the mind of the flesh' in Romans 8:5ff. and by
the 'thoughts' whose 'wills' we used to fulfil as 'children of
wrath' in Ephesians 2:3.[14] Philo's somewhat different language is
probably indebted to the same concept (Williams 1927: 82f.).
Rabbinical theology did not relinquish that tradition, and often
opposed two symmetrical inclinations, evil and good; but it
remained unsystematic, and was hesitant as to the neutrality or
perversion of the *yēṣer hāraʿ,* and on its original implantation.[15]

How deep and strong is the tendency? Augustinians affirm
and Pelagians (or semi-Pelagians) deny that it entails an inability
to turn to the true God. The diagnosis of a bent towards sinning
is closely linked with whatever stand is taken on free will,
whether it is lost or preserved. In this respect, among the Jews,
the Sadducees would appear as the forerunners of Pelagius; the
Essenes would be on the opposite side, and the Pharisees in
between (the 'semi-Pelagians'), if we trust Josephus's well-
balanced model of the three sects.[16] We shall not settle the age-

---

[12] My translation follows the interpretation of André Dupont-Sommer in
Dupont-Sommer and Philonenko 1987: 270, and his restitution of the illegible
word after *yēṣer* (line 16). Another reading, however, would be possible here:
Lohse 1986: 147 suggests one, and translates the second part of the quotation:
'A man is more righteous than another, and a man is more clever than another,
and a (being of) flesh worthier than a form of (clay).' The 'evil inclination' is
also seen in *1 QH* XI.20.

[13] A conjecture mentioned by Porter 1990a: 8f.

[14] See Malina 1969: 25, who draws on W. D. Davies's *Paul and Rabbinic Judaism.*
Eph. 2:3 uses the word *dianoia,* which is the LXX rendering of *yēṣer* in Gn. 8:21
(and 1 Ch. 29:18), the verb *dianoeō* doing the same duty in Gn. 6:5.

[15] So Porter 1990a: 6f. (quoting *b. Yebamoth* 103b: 'When the serpent
copulated with Eve, he infused her with lust'); Williams 1927: 65ff., and, on
the 'defilement' (*inquinamentum*) of Eve, p. 57.

[16] *Wars of the Jews* II.viii.2–14; *Antiquities of the Jews* XIII.v.9; XVIII.i.2–5.

old issue here, but only observe the remarkable force of the language of Scripture. When actual sins (at least) are taken together with the propensity to sin, the Bible speaks plainly of bondage and of the impossibility of change. Jesus himself aroused the anger of his hearers when he insisted that all sinners are slaves to sin (Jn. 8:34), a metaphor which Paul took over and exploited (Rom. 6:19f.). Jeremiah warned his people that they could not do good, any more than an Ethiopian could change his skin or a leopard his spots (Je. 13:23). Paul confirmed that the sinful mind (flesh) does not submit to God's law, 'nor can it do so' (Rom. 8:7), and that human beings left to their own resources (*psychikoi*) cannot understand the things of God (1 Cor. 2:14). No-one can come to the Lord Jesus unless the Father draws or drags (*helkysē*) him or her (Jn. 6:44; *cf.* 65). This suggests that the universal inclination is no superficial trait. On the contrary, it holds a dreadful sway over human life.[17]

Does the bent entail guilt? Since the bent is universal, it is found in those many individuals who are ignorant, or even unconscious, of the divine standards of the good. Do infants deserve condemnation for the propensity which is born in them? Many thinkers are indignant at the mere idea, though it has long been affirmed by the church. Williams (1927: 330) has to invoke 'the crude lights and hard shadows which the burning sun of Africa casts upon its desert sands'[18] to account for Augustine's incredible harshness. Nearer to orthodoxy, and to us in time, David Smith emphatically, though ambiguously, denies that there can be guilt where there is no consciousness of God's standards:

> Children are born innocent, but as they approach
> adolescence they are increasingly able to handle
> abstract ideas, and ultimately, the realisation of sin
> and guilt. It is the awareness of guilt that causes sin to
> kill spiritually . . . When we couple that awareness

---

[17] Pannenberg (1994: 258) offers a perceptive comment on the Pelagian idea of freedom: 'a will that can choose differently when face to face with the norm of the good cannot be in fact a good will. It is more than weak because it is not firmly set upon the good . . . it is already sinful because it is emancipated from commitment to the good.'

[18] On the following page, Williams uses the phrase 'sick souls' of Paul, Augustine, Luther and Newman.

along with Romans 5:12ff., what do we find? Sin is not imputed against innocents. Until there is awareness of guilt (i.e., of breaking the law), the penalty for sin – eternal death – is not imposed. It is evidently covered by the Saviour's atonement (1994: 297f.).[19]

The ambiguity lies in the joint affirmations of innocence and of the role of atonement. If the infant is not to be charged with sin, where does the need for atonement come in? Innocence does not need to be 'covered'. One could also question the correlation of awareness with the handling of abstract ideas. But the main concern is clear, and it finds some echoes in most people's sensitivities: to avoid attaching guilt to tendencies in children or in other morally unconscious persons.

The burden of proof, I suggest, rests with those who would sever the connection between evil inclinations, sin and guilt. Nowhere in Scripture do we see the link between them broken, or even slackened. Guilt is the human correlate of the constant reaction of the absolutely Righteous One, who cannot tolerate the sight of evil. How could the righteous and holy God accept a tendency in human hearts towards the things he abominates, when the first and great commandment is that we should tend towards him with the whole of our hearts and souls and 'intensities'?[20] When James vividly describes the process of temptation (Jas. 1:14f.), he does not deny the sinfulness and guilt of the enticing 'evil desire' (*epithymia*); far from wishing to exonerate the propensity, he brands it as the real culprit. Formally, *epithymia* must be defined as sin, for it breaks the tenth commandment, 'You shall not covet . . .' In Romans 7, Paul in no way suggests that dormant sin could be considered guiltless and remain without charge. 'I lived once' (v. 9) merely expresses his unreliable feeling at the time of his ignorance, not the *truth*

---

[19] Similarly, 'penalty for sin is charged against a person only upon awareness of the law' (p. 369); 'Thus, those who do not reach a point of awareness and accountability are in a state of imputed innocence in which their sins are covered by the finished work of Christ on Calvary. They are one with the saints in belonging to Christ' (p. 371). Suchocki 1994 follows her own path – further from 'evangelical' signposts – to a guiltless sinfulness: 'one can be a sinner "innocently", without guilt, and this applies to infants, small children, and those whose physiological conditions do not allow normal maturation' (p. 129).

[20] This would not be a mistranslation of $m^{e'}\bar{o}\underline{d}$ in Dt. 6:5.

of his state, as if he had enjoyed spiritual life in God's eyes. Rather, the apostle's aim in the passage is to show how the expressed commandment increases what is already the case: sin becomes superlatively sinful, *kath' hyperbolēn hamartōlos* (v. 13).

The presupposition of those who deny 'original guilt' is that guilt requires a distinct and deliberate exercise of personal will. Does Scripture concur? It seems to teach a broader, more inclusive, view. Sins of omission are real sins (Jas. 4:17), and we usually slip into them unawares. Unconscious sins need divine forgiveness (Ps. 19:12) and may come under God's judgment (1 Cor. 4:4). Unintentional sins must be atoned for, as the law of Numbers 15:27ff. stipulates; the Septuagint used the word *akousioi* here, corresponding to 'unintentional', as Turretin noticed (1847: 537 [IX.2.4]). (Heb. 10:26 distinguishes deliberate [*ekousiōs*] sin as just one sort of sinning.) Turretin also refers to Romans 7:16: the fact that the man does what he does not want to do does not excuse him; it only adds to his wretchedness under the condemnation of the law.

The biblical witness, then, taken at face value, associates bondage and guilt with the universal bent of humankind. This deserves to be called *sin* with the full force of the word.

Natural sinfulness

If sinfulness is universal in humankind, and present 'from youth', should it be predicated of human *nature*? The Augustinian dogma does take that apparently natural step, and not without predecessors. Philo frequently used cognates of the Greek word 'nature' (*physis*) to stress the impregnation of evil; he stigmatized the 'adulterous nature' and spoke of the 'innate [or, co-natural] evils of our race', and of 'sinning innate [or, co-natural] in everyone who is born'.[21] Even earlier, the apocryphal book of Wisdom refers to the Canaanites' malice as *emphytos*: implanted in them, part of their nature. It speaks of their 'genesis' as evil, and to their seed (*sperma*) as accursed (12:10f.).

---

[21] '*Hē mochthēra physis*', in *De confusione linguarum* 17; '*ta symphyta kaka tou genous hēmōn*', in *Quis rerum divinarum heres sit* 55; '*panti gennētō . . . symphyes to hamartanein*', in *De vita Mosis* 2.147, as gleaned from Williams 1927: 83 n. 2 and other writers.

Does canonical Scripture agree? The actual word 'nature' is found once with reference to guilt or liability to divine wrath: 'We were by nature [*physei*] children of wrath' (Eph. 2:3). Several have attempted to loosen the Augustinian grip on this remarkable 'proof-text'. Didymus of Alexandria (*c.* 311–396) reduces the meaning to 'really, in truth',[22] but the antithetical term which one would then expect (something like 'but according to appearances we were . . .') is totally absent. Others oppose 'by nature' to the phrase 'by grace', several verses later (v. 8). But that reading sounds somewhat anachronistic, betraying the influence of the later 'nature–grace' conceptual scheme. By far the most attractive exegesis connects the word with the apostle's theme in the whole chapter, indeed in the whole development of Ephesians 1 – 3: that of Jews and non-Jews made one.[23] *Physei* refers to ethnic origin, birth, and lineage, just as it does in a close parallel passage, Galatians 2:15. 'Nature', therefore, does not bear the precise technical meaning given to the term by philosophers or later theologians, but the implications are essentially the same as those of the church doctrine. The whole emphasis of the paragraph points to the same interpretation, as Ramm (1985: 45f.) skilfully brings out: we were children of wrath, sons of disobedience, dead in trespasses and sins, and led by the tendencies (*thelēmata*) of the flesh.

The use of the loaded term 'flesh' provides powerful support for the concept of 'natural' sinfulness. Indisputably, the word frequently approximates to 'human nature', while a related meaning evokes kinship or family ties. The link between 'flesh' and guilty propensities to evil is significant for doctrine. This link is not obvious in the Old Testament, despite the term's connotations of frailty, transitoriness and vulnerability, and whatever might be suggested by Genesis 6:4, 'for he is flesh' – an enigmatic text. In Qumran, the *Community Rule* prescribes the striking confession, 'I belong to wicked humankind, to the

---

[22] I owe the quotation from Didymus' *Contra Manicheos*, ch. 3, to M. Jean de Savignac, in a personal letter.

[23] Weighty names might be listed in favour of this interpretation, *e.g.* Ligier 1961: 286ff., especially 288f. and n. 147; Bruce 1984: *ad loc.*; and O'Brien 1994: 132, who maintains the prominence of the Jews–Gentiles theme (against some recent interpreters, n. 4), and speaks (p. 137) of 'our fallen, self-centred human nature'.

communion [*sôd*] of sinful flesh.'[24] Paul's extraordinary development of the idea, whereby the flesh becomes the seat and
power of indwelling sin, even the hypostasis of sin's tyranny,
maintains continuity with previous usage; 'being fleshly'
(*sarkikoi*) equals 'walking in the human way' (*kata anthrōpon*)
and 'being human beings' (1 Cor. 3:3f.). This language
describes the fact that human nature *concretely* is at enmity with
God; hence the meaning attached to 'flesh'.[25] Johannine usage
is not far removed from this; Jesus' word in John 3:6,
contrasting flesh born of flesh with kingdom requirements,
does imply a radical human inadequacy and inability in
spiritual matters. Berkouwer (1971: 488) underestimates the
import of that verse, failing to notice that our Lord refers to
birth or conception (*gennaō*) to account for the prevailing state
of affairs – not to the event of birth as such, but as signifying
the transmission of human nature. The mention of birth is not
incidental, since the conversation with Nicodemus focuses on
that very theme.

Other passages are interested in the question of the origin of
sin in the individual. Job 14:4 does not require the amplification
of the Vulgate, 'Who can make pure what was conceived of
impure seed?', to point in a direction similar to that of the
passages just discussed (so Nicole 1986: *ad loc.*). Job 15:14 and
25:4 echo the same thought, almost proverbial in tone. The
mother's ritual impurity (Lv. 12:2ff.) may be in the background;
it would then function as a symbol of that sinfulness that adheres
to nature as it is transmitted.[26]

The *locus classicus* is Psalm 51:6. A literal rendering could
read: 'Indeed, in [or, with] iniquity was I born, and in [with]
sin was my mother warm of me.' Two misguided interpretations may be put aside without further ado. First, virtually no-
one today follows Augustine in viewing the procreative act as
sinful *per se* (in our fallen condition). Such a view finds no

[24] *1 QS* XI:9; *cf. 1 QH* XV:21: 'How can flesh have the intelligence (of your works) . . .?' and IX:16 already quoted above.
[25] 'The creature as subsisting in distinction from God has become practically equivalent to creature opposing itself to God; and *sarx*, which marks creature-ship, connotes also its invariable empirical accompaniment of *hamartia*', writes William P. Dickson (1883: 320) in conclusion of his analysis, a study still unsurpassed in my view.
[26] See the thought-provoking comments of Kristeva 1980.

support anywhere else in Scripture, and the synonymous parallelism of the verse contradicts the idea, since the delivery of the child ('I was born') could not be considered sinful even in Augustinian eyes. Secondly, those who would charge the psalmist's mother with a specific sin, such as adultery or promiscuity, are on no surer ground. The only argument of Maillot and Lelièvre (1966: 12f., 22) is based on the highly negative connotation of the verb 'being warm', perhaps 'being in heat' (*yāḥam*). But this is merely hypothetical, with only two other occurrences (Gn. 30:41; 31:10), and is criticized by able linguists.[27] There is not a shred of evidence to suggest that David's mother had misbehaved, and if one doubts the authenticity of the psalm's superscription, the fact remains that Israelites ascribed its language to David and recited the psalm as a common confession. Ligier's sophisticated version, which identifies the 'mother' with the generation of the exile, or even with Jehoiachin's mother (on the basis of Je. 22:26), suffers from the same deficiencies and fails to carry conviction.[28] Luther had rightly observed that the text does *not* say: 'My mother sinned when she conceived me' (quoted by Berkouwer 1971: 535 n. 178). David is not trying to accuse his mother in order to excuse himself! Actually, mentioning the mother follows the rules of Mediterranean rhetoric, whether in abuse of others or in humble reference to oneself: 'Your handmaid's son' just means 'Your servant'. David confesses his own sinfulness, in a spirit of true repentance.

Far from attempting to downplay his guilt, David refers to his birth and conception in the clear realization that his very being is shot through and through with the tendencies that produced the fruits of adultery and murder. As far back as he can go, he sees his life as sinful. Therefore, this radical confession issues in his request for purification in the innermost parts of his person (v. 7). Even the 'man according to the LORD's heart' has to acknowledge that he is corrupt and guilty 'by nature', like others

---

[27] Margot 1979: 64 severely chides Maillot and Lelièvre.

[28] See Ligier 1960: 131 (with n. 180), 134ff., 150. The key to the meaning of the verse, he claims, is the comparison with Is. 57:3ff. (post-exilic); but he does not explain that the verb is *ḥāmam* rather than *yāḥam* if there is an allusion; he also neglects the fact that the metaphorical use of 'mother' for the community always goes with children in the *plural*, and that is not the case in Ps. 51.

– like the wicked who are wayward 'from birth', 'from the womb' (Ps. 58:3).[29]

In addition, we may recall once more Jeremiah's comparison (13:23) of his fellow countrymen's expertise in the practice of sin with an Ethiopian's colour of skin and a leopard's spots – both 'natural' features. It is striking, too, that Jesus deliberately works back from the fruits to the nature of the tree (Mt. 7:16ff.; 12:33; cf. Jas. 3:12); he denounces 'broods[30] of vipers' and makes 'being evil' the cause of the foul talk from which there is no escape (Mt. 12:34). Melanchthon argued forcefully that the apostolic description of actual sins as 'the *fruits* of sin' indicates that original sin is what determines human nature.[31] It would be difficult biblically to countenance the rather bold counter-position of Trent: 'This concupiscence, *which sometimes the Apostle calls sin* [Rom. 6:12ff.], the Holy Council declares that the Catholic Church has never understood to be called sin because it is, in the regenerate, *truly and properly* sin, but because it stems from sin and inclines to sin.'[32]

At the same time, Scripture can marvel at the beauty and wisdom evident in the way the human being is constituted: 'I praise you because I am fearfully and wonderfully made; your works are wonderful' (Ps. 139:14, NIV). The provocative sage

[29] A majority of scholars have discerned the meaning of Ps. 51:6. See, *e.g.*, Scharbert 1968: 91, who also quotes from Eichrodt, and stresses the original character of the Israelite view. Edwards 1879:143 offers a quote from Aben[Ibn]-Ezra as an epigraph: 'Because of concupiscence, innate in the human heart, it is said, "I was born in iniquity"; the meaning is that, from birth, the *yēṣer hārāʿ*, the evil formation, is implanted in the human heart' (my translation from Latin). Peters (1994: 25) goes far in the direction of the doctrine of original sin: 'The reference [in Ps. 51] is not to one of the Psalmist's mother's indiscretions. The reference is rather to the situation of sin into which we all are born, symbolized as a contagion that has been passed down not only through three or four prior generations (Exod. 20:5) but all the way back to the father and mother of the race.'

[30] The word is *gennēma*. The question could be raised whether the word *genea*, which Jesus often used (and together with the predicate 'evil'), carries, for him, a similar meaning. Ligier's investigation (1961: 124, 129f.) leads him to a cautious negative verdict, though Mt. 17:17 recalls Dt. 32:20.

[31] Melanchthon, *Loci communes theologici*, art. *Peccatum*, 1, as quoted (translated into French) by Frost 1975a: 101 n. 29.

[32] *Fifth Canon on Original Sin*, quoted by Frost 1975b: 74 (my italics). My translation (from the Latin text in Denzinger's *Enchiridion*) is less bold than the one used by Frost.

Qōhelet agrees: 'God made humankind upright . . .' (Ec. 7:29). Nature, in the strict sense of what makes men and women human, the essence of being a particular kind of creature, cannot be termed evil. The phrase 'natural sinfulness' conceals a paradox, which Tertullian (*De anima* 41) noticed ('The corruption of nature is another nature').[33] Calvin deliberately developed this thought: 'We say, then, that man is corrupted by a natural viciousness, but not one which proceeded from nature' (*Institutes* II.i.11). Sinfulness has become our quasi-nature while remaining truly our anti-nature.

Inherited sinfulness

Are the quasi-nature and anti-nature of sin *inherited* in the same way as nature? John 3:6 ('What is born of the flesh is flesh' and cannot see the kingdom of God) and kindred passages strongly suggest a positive answer. Flesh begets flesh. This is the law of heredity, and one could expect it to apply when 'flesh' takes on a sinful aspect. Transmission from forebears is mentioned once (the futility of life being one of the faces of sin; 1 Pet. 1:18); but the word used there (*patroparadotos*) may suggest social rather than biological modes of inheritance.

Further evidence pointing to the hereditary transmission of sinfulness may be found in the strategy of prophetic rebuke. Indictments often follow the pattern: 'You are truly the children of your parents . . .' tracing perversity back to the ancestors of the accused. Hosea castigates his fellow Israelites by recalling Jacob's deviousness from his mother's womb and up to the mysterious nocturnal fight at Peniel (Ho. 12:3f.; the mention of Jacob's tears, however, may suggest his conversion there, an example for his descendants to follow). Hosea contrasts Jacob's behaviour with the Lord's action through his prophet Moses, which illustrated Israel's perennial opposition to God's designs and to his prophetic agents (12:12f. – Jacob left the land, God through Moses brought Israel back to the land; Jacob had to do hard service and care for sheep, Israel under Moses enjoys the benefit of being cared for). Isaiah makes the blunt charge: 'Your first father sinned', a fact that shows the falsity of the people's

---

[33] Liébaert 1975: 54 quotes Cyril of Alexandria, who said that humanity's fallen condition is both 'natural' and *para physin* (contrary to nature).

case (Is. 43:27); most commentators think Jacob is the father, but some see a reference to Abraham, and Alexander (1953: *ad loc.*) to Adam, the very first patriarch.[34] Ezekiel insists on the racial connection, reminding Jerusalem that 'Your mother was a Hittite and your father an Amorite', and quoting the proverb 'Like mother, like daughter' (16:44ff.). Scharbert too (1968: 80ff.) has noticed the phenomenon; in addition to Ezekiel 16, he quotes Hosea 9:10; 10:9; Amos 2:4, 7; Isaiah 1:4; Jeremiah 2:17; 11:6ff. (9:12ff.). He also mentions the curse which rests on some family lines, such as Eli's (see 1 Ki. 2:27, referring back to 1 Sa. 2:30–35) (p. 87). One cannot miss the idea of inherited sinfulness in the Old Testament.

At the same time, Scripture draws back from the rhetoric of traditional theology.[35] Nowhere does it approach such crude expressions as Anselm's: 'Of leprous parents, lepers are born; the same of our first parents.'[36] Nowhere does it reduce the transmission to such narrow terms as in David Smith's bold language: 'We may assume, then, that each infant born into the world possesses that gene, as it were, that predisposes toward sin' (1994: 369), comparable to genes that would predispose to shyness, alcoholism, depression, or to the HIV virus (p. 371). Writing of the so-called 'Yahwist', Scharbert stresses that 'the guilt of humankind is not for him a merely biological, but even more an ethical, datum' (1968: 76). Turretin emphasized that 'the mere *law of nature*, after which, as man begets man and the leprous begets the leprous, corrupt man begets corrupt man' is not enough to safeguard the truth and justice of sin's propagation (1847: 562 [IX.9.21], my

[34] Alexander adds: 'At the same time it may be considered as implied, that all their fathers who had since lived shared in the original depravity, and thus the same sense is obtained that would have been expressed by the collective explanation of *first father*.' Motyer (1993: *ad loc.*) considers all three names possible. Although I believe Jacob to be more probable, a word may be said in favour of a fourth name, according to the rare choice of the *Bible annotée: ad loc.* – Aaron, since the parallel clauses are directed to priestly dignitaries.

[35] 'Like begets like' is a common phrase in a recent scholarly treatment, Garlington 1994: 82, 86 n. 58, 100, 107. Without wishing to deny the truth and relevance of the statement, its application to the riddle of original sin is perhaps too quick and complacent, as if it were a simple key to unlock the complexity of the issue.

[36] Anselm, *De conceptu virginali et originali peccato* 2, as quoted (my translation) by Brunner 1947: 121 n. 2.

translation). His reservations reflect the distinctive restraint of Scripture.

Adamic sinfulness

Since forebears are brought into the dock when the prophets denounce the people's sins, what about Adam (and Eve)? Does Scripture trace the corruption of nature back to Adam? Is he singled out for a special role?

Two passages, Genesis 3 and Romans 5:12ff., play such an important role in this debate that I shall devote a chapter each to a fuller study of their logic and intention. Here, however, we must be content, provisionally, with a quick sketch of a possible answer.

Several critics deny that these passages can bear the weight in biblical thought that Augustine has placed upon them. They argue from the lack of echoes and references elsewhere in Scripture, and try to minimize their doctrinal importance. Paul Ricœur (1967: 237f.) brilliantly summarizes this position: 'In every way the addition [of Adam] is belated and, in certain respects, non-essential . . . The Prophets ignore him . . . Jesus himself never refers to the Adamic story.' As to Romans 5, it is an artificial construction; Paul is really interested in Christ, not in Adam; he contrives a homiletical symmetry, but Adam's part constitutes 'only a flying buttress', 'only a false column' (p. 239).

These arguments look formidable, but they can be unmasked as paper tigers. Scharbert (1968:19) incisively criticizes the current opinion (*e.g.* Lohfink's) about the 'isolation' of Genesis 3 in the Old Testament. With Vriezen, he maintains the validity of the traditional interpretation of the chapter.[37] Even if the Bible contained no echoes at all of that passage, frequency of occurrence could not be the sole measure of importance; its place in the canon is significant. It is obvious that the Eden story is no peripheral anecdote or marginal addition; it belongs decisively to the structure of Genesis and to that of the Torah. It has a major aetiological intention, with the following chapters showing the results of the inaugural tragedy, and chapter 11 recounting a kind of socio-political duplication of that tragedy after the flood (similarities in language between Genesis 3 and

[37] He also appeals to W. Eichrodt's support (pp. 13ff.)

the Babel story are striking). Turretin (1847: 571 [IX.10.8])
appealed to Genesis 5:3 as implying the change from divine to
Adamic likeness.

Beyond Genesis, allusions to Adam's fateful action are by no
means impossible to find. An ear finely attuned to Scripture
does detect distinct echoes of it. Using source-critical labels (in
which I would not follow him), Scharbert (1968: 12) sees
allusions to Adam in the Yahwist, the Elohist, the Priestly
Document, the Deuteronomist, the Chronicler and Jesus ben
Sirach (Ecclesiasticus). We shall review other pieces of evidence
in the Prophets and the Writings. Suffice it for the moment to
point to Clemens's (1994: 5ff.) recent interpretation of the book
of Ecclesiastes as almost a 'commentary' on Genesis 1 – 3.[38]

In Judaism, the Old Testament seeds of the doctrine began to
germinate, although the import of the Eden story was eclipsed
for a time by explanations based on Genesis 6 (the 'angelic
watcher' theory).[39] The responsibility of Adam or Eve was
affirmed, mostly regarding death, but also regarding the cause
of corruption and 'fallenness'. Among the books of the
Apocrypha, Wisdom and Ecclesiasticus focus on two of the
Genesis 3 protagonists; Wisdom 2:23f. teaches that 'it was the
devil's spite that brought death into the world' (NEB) – and
Williams himself has to acknowledge here 'an embryonic
doctrine of Original Sin' (1927: 55). Ecclesiasticus 25:24
expresses the author's misogyny: 'Woman is the origin of sin,
and it is through her that we all die' (NEB). The Qumran hymn
quoted earlier provides a remarkable reference to the 'first
transgression', *peša' rîšôn*: 'I was comforted regarding the first
transgression.'[40] Despite its strong and familiar emphasis on free
will and the responsibility of each individual (54:19 and, earlier,
15), *2 Baruch* sees our first parents as the fountain-head of
corruption and death; Adam plunged 'many' into darkness
(18:2; 56:8f.) and brought death upon humankind (23:4; 54:15).
There is pathos in the question put to him:

---

[38] This article is highly suggestive, even if one might wish to remain more
cautious.

[39] Williams 1927: 19ff. insists on its great influence in Judaism and (p. 114) on
that influence lingering in Jewish Christianity.

[40] *1 QH* IX:13, following Dupont-Sommer's (1987) understanding; Lohse
1986: 147 again differs ('*die frühere Sünde*', 'the earlier sin').

O Adam, what hast thou done to all those who are
  born of thee?
And what will be said to the first Eve who hearkened to
  the Serpent?
For all this multitude are going to corruption;
Nor is there any numbering of those whom the fire
  devours (48:42–43).[41]

4 Ezra (= *2 Esdras*) goes even further, raising Adam's responsibility for human death and unrighteousness to a position of crucial importance. 'For a grain of evil seed was sown in Adam's heart from the beginning, and how much ungodliness it has produced . . .' (4:30).[42] And the lament is more consistent than in *2 Baruch*'s case:

O Adam, what have you done? For though it was you
who sinned, this fall was not yours alone, but ours also
who are your descendants [*qui ex te advenimus*]. For
what good is it to us, if an eternal age has been
promised to us, but we have done deeds that bring
death? (*4 Ezra* 7:118f.)[43]

Such utterances warrant the conclusion that ideas of 'original sin' were probably not totally foreign to the New Testament Jewish context. Against the background they provide, possible allusions in the New Testament gain probability; we may be right to see echoes of this material in them.

There are possible allusions and echoes of the Paradise story in the New Testament – more than many imagine. Since the next chapter will attempt to sift the evidence for relevant data, it will be sufficient to state here that even the synoptic gospels are not devoid of traces of interest in the Genesis origin of sinfulness; Jesus' comments on divorce are impressive in this regard. The Johannine corpus contains several major references to the Eden drama, although they focus on protagonists other than the first couple. Paul's letters reveal on many occasions (in

[41] De Vries's translation, 1962: 368b.
[42] As quoted in De Vries 1962: 369a.
[43] As quoted in De Vries 1962: 369a. See also 7:68 (quoted on p. 369b): 'For all who have been born are involved in iniquities, and are full of sins and burdened with transgressions'.

addition to Rom. 5) that Genesis 3 was on his mind. In his discussion of the way in which Paul uses the passage, Williams states that it may be 'safely inferred from St. Paul's confident assumption of the Adam-doctrine . . . that *no other theory of the origin of evil was in possession of the Gentile-Christian field* at the time when he wrote'.[44]

We may therefore confidently pass over the pessimistic evaluations of various scholars. Romans 5 is no isolated monument, and certainly not a 'false column' in the temple of biblical teaching.

Yet we can readily concur that the apostle's elaboration of the magnitude of Adam's role far exceeds any other reference to Genesis 3, both within and without the Scriptures. His discernment is a gift of divine inspiration, and it offers us an example of rigorous, sober, responsible yet daring inventiveness in fulfilling the theologian's calling. Anselm spoke of *fides quaerens intellectum* ('faith seeking understanding'); the theologian thinks through and between revealed truths, in the service of the whole truth. We are called to emulate Paul's example, though our sketching of truth is fallible and imperfect. But we have the gracious promise that the Spirit who inspired him will assist us in our task.

[44] Williams 1927: 117 (italics his); on pp. 119f., Williams speculates about a possible Galilean provenance of that belief.

Chapter Two

Original sin as Adamic event

Traditionally, the church has distinguished between *originated* original sin (that tendency to sinfulness with which we are born) and the *originating* original sin (the transgression Adam perpetrated in the Garden and through which sin and death invaded our world).[1] The affirmation of the disobedience in Eden as a real event or occurrence at a specific moment in time has been part of church dogma from the start; this could hardly be disputed.[2] I submit that it is an *essential* part, which we shall be wise to maintain. This, however, sounds hopelessly conservative and literalistic to many ears today, not only among opponents of the doctrine of original sin but among its official defenders, especially Roman Catholic and 'neo-orthodox'.

Three factors, in connection with fact, text and meaning, work together to undermine or to overthrow earlier beliefs regarding Adam's originating sin.

First, the pressure of scientific opinion regarding human origins weighs heavily on our debate. Both the framework of evolutionary theory and the specific reconstruction based on fossil findings, with the series stretching from *homo habilis* to *homo sapiens sapiens* (first palaeolithic and then neolithic), are inimical to the representation of a first man's 'fall' from perfection so many millennia ago. Williams (1927: 513ff.) often bows before current Darwinian perspectives, although he helpfully criticizes F. R. Tennant's reduction of 'sinfulness' to 'anachronism' in evolution's progress (pp. 530–531). Brunner takes it for granted that the Eden narrative 'is no longer historically credible' and has lost all 'convincing power' (1947:

---

[1] Grelot (1973: 13) introduces *originaire*, 'originary,' for the fateful event of our human origins.

[2] Liébaert (1975: 37, 47) recognizes the fact in patristic exegesis, though the fathers escape excessive literalism; only in Origen's school is there a significant departure from the natural or naïve historical.

37

120; *cf.* 1952: 48–49, 74). Paul Ricœur departs from his usual caution to declare: 'What we know, as men of science, about the beginnings of mankind leaves no place for such a primordial event' (1967: 235). Similar quotations could be added *ad libitum.*[3] Bernard Ramm (1985: 63) aptly borrows the phrase, in that sense, 'the death of Adam'.[4]

Secondly, conclusions of critical-literary study work against the credibility of the older understanding. The language of Genesis 2 and 3, we are told, takes us into the world of aetiological myths: a man fashioned from clay, wonderful trees bearing magical fruits, a serpent, or rather *the* Serpent, naturally gifted with speech (and craftiness). All these are typical products of the mythopoeic imagination. They signal the genre of our narrative: a story, but not history, a beautiful myth (or, at least, saga) trimmed to suit monotheism. The very name 'Adam', which means 'humankind' collectively, should warn us off the wrong track of a naïve historical reading. The argument (as we saw) is buttressed by a very negative estimate of the influence of the Genesis narrative on the rest of Scripture; the alleged lack of references and allusions is held to point to a marginal status, whereas an 'Augustinian' type of reading confers on it a major dogmatic importance.

Thirdly, at the reflective level, the claim is put forward that the meaning, the *intentio,* of the passage is better preserved, better promoted, indeed liberated, if we break it loose from a contingent, local accident. It is faith that compels us to purge the doctrine of bygone days of a misguided historical reference (as Brunner insists; 1947: 20). Ricœur, who never tires of extolling his hermeneutics of symbols, as the way out of the fundamentalism-rationalism dilemma,[5] claims that the meaning of the Genesis story 'appears only if we completely renounce projecting the Adamic figure into history . . .' (1974: 284). Here he departs from his accustomed courtesy in debate and derides the orthodox interpretation: 'An old peculiar gentleman, all alone with his wife in a garden, who is supposed to have

---

[3] *E.g.* Martelet 1986: 37; the older construction 'could only collapse before the scientific knowledge that was to be gained of the living world'.

[4] Ramm borrows from John C. Greene's title, *The Death of Adam: Evolution and its Impact on Western Thought* (Ames, Ia.: Iowa State University Press, 1959).

[5] Ricœur 1974: 285: 'Between the naive historicism of fundamentalism and the bloodless moralism of rationalism the way of hermeneutics opens up.'

transmitted by means of physical generation his own most private nastiness' (1964: 115). Modern theologians are wont to praise meaning at the expense of historical reference.[6]

This chapter deals with the issues in theologically centripetal order: from the outer circle to the heart of the matter.

The Eden story and palaeo-anthropology

Faithfully obeying the *sola Scriptura* rule, the 'formal principle' of the Reformers, Christians dare refuse modern scientific knowledge a *constitutive* role in the interpretation of biblical texts;[7] but a fideistic separation between science and faith betrays the biblical sense of truth. Once instructed by the sovereign Word of God, our faith responsibly welcomes whatever information, drawn from God's 'general revelation', holds proper credentials. Hence it would be unwise to discount, on *a priori* grounds, current views of humankind's remotest past.[8]

Without pretending to more authority than an amateur reader can wield in palaeo-anthropology and related fields, I nevertheless venture the opinion that the judgments quoted above lack due caution and reserve. Actually, they depart from scientific rigour and slip into a more ideological area. We must remain open to evidence. The theory of evolution, when it is not expanded to philosophical dimensions, does not raise insuperable objections from the point of view of evangelical theology. Yet, as a large and flexible 'paradigm' or macro-model, it is incapable of formal proof. It has shown itself able to deal with a great many difficulties, but many others (some at decisive

---

[6] On this see Blocher 1989.

[7] I would still resist the arguments put forward by Lucas (1987: 46–51); neither would I entirely follow his reading of Calvin (on Ps. 58:5).

[8] A worthy defender of the essential historicity of the fall, Schönborn (1991b) seems to lack confidence here. He stresses that figurative language in Gn. 2 – 3 tells of a 'reality' (*Wirklichkeit*) which 'is not simply mythical', but which 'we cannot reach by rational, empirical, historical ways' (p. 75). Adam and Eve, whose real existence we must affirm, 'we do not find in archaeology' (p. 93). Of course, this may be accepted in a merely 'technical' sense, and Schönborn may only be looking for apologetic protection; however, considering the fideistic temptation, this chapter will attempt to face the difficult connection with paleontology more boldly.

methodological levels) have not been solved.[9] The theory of evolution should not be imposed as a dogma.

Nearest to the Adamic problem – 'Adam, where art thou?' – the prehistoric *homo* series still undergoes periodic revision. 'Hard' evidence is available only for a limited number of fixed points. There are enough gaps in the evidence to render unwise any assertion that our science leaves no place for Eden. Just as we deny worshipping a 'God of the gaps', however, I do not wish to salvage a mere 'Adam of the gaps'. But my preference must not set the final rule. Our present state of knowledge, or, rather, of ignorance, *may* mean that being satisfied with a provisional solution of that kind is the wiser course, the expression of humble trust, in hope.

Actually, there are several schemes that would provide a minimal reconciliation between the Genesis record and reliable scientific theory.[10] The most attractive, or the least unsatisfactory – for it is not free of tensions – seems to be the solution advocated by John J. Davis (1980: 137ff.). It requires a non-literal interpretation of the *fourth* chapter of Genesis, with the story spanning tens of millennia and the genealogical links being understood as they would be in the following 'digest' of European history: 'Caesar begat Charlemagne, who begat Napoleon.' The account starts with the emergence of *homo sapiens sapiens*, some 40,000 years ago, this *homo* type being identified as 'Adamic'. This ensures continuity with present humankind, which is likely to have proceeded from a unique centre.[11] It leads to the typical neolithic situation, about thirty millennia later; as a popular summary of neolithic culture, Genesis 4 could hardly be bettered.

[9] Denton 1985 offers the most effective critique I have read, without overstepping the boundaries of natural science. Johnson 1991 (a professor of law) builds upon Denton's contribution, but with overt Christian motivations.

[10] I briefly looked at them in Blocher 1984, in the appendix on 'Scientific Hypotheses and the Beginning of Genesis'. This was a shortened version of the French original, especially on the delicate Adamic issue. In the second French edition (*Révélation des origines: Le début de la Genèse*, Lausanne: Presses Bibliques Universitaires, 1988), this part was updated and amplified.

[11] Scientific opinion has been wavering on this issue. We may safely consider *monophyletism* (origin in one definite line) as a strongly supported position, and *monogenism* (origin in one couple) as impossible to disprove – indeed, as actually encouraged by distinct scientific considerations such as those put forward by Lejeune 1968: 191, according to Ruffié 1983: 292.

I have shown elsewhere that the second major section of Genesis (2:4 – 3:24) makes use of pictorial, symbolic language as it recounts the story of origins, and this requires a departure from a rigid literal reading. Does the same obtain in the case of Genesis 4? A marked change in tone or register is perceptible; we may not simply extend our findings regarding the Paradise chapters to the brief narrative which follows them. Yet there are textual pointers to redactional unity. Genesis 4:16, 'East of Eden', refers us back to the preceding section. The use of the same words, ('desire' and 'domination'), one of them rather rare, in both 3:16 and 4:7 is a striking and probably significant 'coincidence'. The total number of occurrences of the divine names 'God' and 'LORD' in the first four chapters is seventy. This is not accidental. We should not miss the indication that Genesis 1 – 4 is, as a whole, an introductory or foundational 'book of origins',[12] coming before 'the written account of Adam's line' (NIV) set out in 5:1ff. It is permissible therefore not to identify the narrative with straightforward, ordinary history, and to look for another historical genre: that of a well-crafted, childlike drawing of the far-distant past, with illustrative and typological interests uppermost – something like the images carved on the tympans of Romanesque cathedrals and the stories told by their stained-glass windows.

If this flexible approach be allowed, and provided we avoid fanciful exaggerations of the privileges of innocence, it does not prove overly difficult to fit Adam, as the first 'theological man' and the progenitor of *sapiens sapiens*, into the schemes of palaeo-anthropology. Obviously, fossil remains can tell us nothing of his first 'estate', local and ephemeral as it was. Objections raised in the name of the cultural requirements for such a great spiritual choice (Heddebaut 1975: 157ff.) – which the first *sapiens sapiens* is supposed not to have met – lack full cogency. Modern prejudice may tempt us to underestimate the mental powers and sensitivities of palaeolithic man; the artists who painted the cave walls of Lascaux, Altamira, and the Grotte Chauvet near Vallon-Pont-d'Arc, discovered in December 1994, were masters at least equal to the greatest in our times. How do we measure

[12] See also vv. 20f., and implicitly 22. Play on names (Cain, Abel, Nod, Seth), though far from exceptional in Old Testament 'historical' writing, may also suggest stylized storytelling.

culture? We should, moreover, beware of presupposing too close a link between cultural refinement and spiritual competence. Who are we to pass judgment on these matters? C. S. Lewis (1940: 67) insisted that poor technical capacities were no indication of deeper moral-personal abilities; even children reach profound understandings. Though we feel uncomfortable with all the uncertainties when we try to correlate scientific data and the results of a sensible interpretation of Genesis 1 – 4, therefore, we may maintain as plausible the hypothesis that the biblical Adam and Eve were the first parents of our race, some 40,000 years ago; and we may posit an initial period of fellowship with God in their lives before they apostatized.

The Eden story and biblical inter-textuality

Inter-textuality refers to echoes of a passage in later writings, which also witness to its *Wirkungsgeschichte*, the history of the effects it produced; that is, of the living process it set in motion. In biblical interpretation, inter-textuality provides invaluable help; the symphony of echoes, in the one inspired corpus, accompanies the 'analogy of faith', the rule of rules in Reformation hermeneutics. This is why the issue raised by critics who allege the silence of the rest of Scripture (apart from Rom. 5) on the content of Genesis 3 is of supreme moment for evangelical readers. Earlier I challenged, in preliminary fashion, the argument which tends to rob the Genesis narrative of its 'Augustinian' importance. The time has come to scrutinize the matter a little more.

Silence may be eloquent – some arguments *e silentio* carry much weight – but not always. How can we be sure that our prejudices have not dulled our sense of hearing? Granted, the number of references to Genesis 3 does not match the expectations of most modern readers, but how justified are these expectations themselves? The genre and setting of Old Testament discourse might well account for the phenomena, as Scharbert claims (1968: 19). I have mentioned the fine balance of canonical arrangement, which raises to prominence the opening chapters of the Bible even in the absence of explicit references by other books. As to Romans 5, some comments sound suspiciously like lame attempts to rob the apostle's language of its force; it obviously takes much rhetoric to reduce

Paul's argument to mere rhetoric. Paucity of references, apart from Romans 5, is insufficient ground for reducing the importance this passage confers upon the story of Eden, together with its canonical pride of place.

But I am not ready to concede the premise that the references are few. Denying the presence of echoes throughout Scripture does not accurately represent the data. Far from there being a mere handful, there are in fact many relevant passages.

In the Old Testament, apart from correspondences in the outline of Genesis,[13] many allusions may be detected in the Prophets and in the Writings, especially the wisdom literature. 'The prophets', Ligier claims, 'are more familiar with the themes of Genesis than many imagine' (1960: 154), and he perceives echoes in Hosea, Amos, Micah, Isaiah, and the 'prophetic' warning of Deuteronomy 30:18 (pp. 159, 208).[14] Hosea 6:7, 'Like Adam, they have broken the covenant' (NIV), is an old proof-text, and not the weaker for that.[15] Modern Jewish scholars still feel confident about that way of reading the verse,[16] and we do observe in Genesis 2 all the essential ingredients of covenant.

Are there clear traces in Amos and Micah? In all frankness, I

---

[13] In addition to the symmetry between Gn. 3 and 11 (almost an *inclusio* for the pre-Abrahamic survey), one could study the correspondence with Gn. 9. After the Flood – 'de-creation' – the restoration resembles a new creation, and parallels to Gn. 1 signal that theme (apart from bloodshed, sin has already entered the world, *cf.* 8:21); Noah's drunkenness and Ham's shameless behaviour may then be connected with Gn. 3 – 4, echoing the themes of nakedness to be covered, and of antithetical destinies for brothers and their seeds. (One recalls also that Abelard thought that the tree of knowledge of good and evil was the vine, the fruit of which deceitfully opens the eyes of men, and deludes them into thinking that they transcend good and evil.)

[14] The grammatical structure is the same as in Gn. 2:17, but not the verb ('*perish* you shall perish'); this makes Ligier's suggestion less persuasive.

[15] Warfield 1970a puts forward a persuasive and moderate plea in favour of the 'Adam' understanding; in support, he is able to cite many names, including Cyril of Jerusalem, Jerome, Rashi, Abarbanel and Luther, and among modern scholars J. Orr, H. Bavinck and G. Vos (p. 129).

[16] Ligier (1960: 153 n. 25) quotes Robert Gordis; and the *Bible du rabbinat* (1899: *ad loc.*) indicates that it was Rashi's interpretation. Also in favour, among modern evangelicals, are J. Barton Payne (1962: 92, 215) and, cautiously, O. Palmer Robertson (1980: 17–25).

fail to perceive them.[17] But when we turn to Isaiah, with its thematic context of creation and its 'Paradise regained' atmosphere (*cf.* 11:5ff.), the promise that the serpent shall eat dust (65:25) distinctly recalls the verdict of Genesis 3:14. Implicitly, all the evils that shall at last be forgotten in the newly created Jerusalem (vv. 16ff.) are traced back to the original serpent's manoeuvre, for which he was sentenced to dust.

Ezekiel likes to play with the memory of Eden. On several occasions, he shows remarkable freedom in his allusions to Genesis; the trees of Eden now represent the powerful nations or potentates of the day (31:7–9, 16–18). The river flowing from the eschatological temple (Ezk. 47) should be identified as the original River, before it divided into the powerful Tigris, the Euphrates, probably the Nile and possibly the Indus rivers. The wonderful trees associated with it bring us back into Paradise, and John's Revelation (22:2) expressly confirms this, since they receive the name 'the tree of life'. The major passage for our purposes is the ironic dirge over the death and fall of the king of Tyre (Ezk. 28:12–19). The use of Eden language here implies more than mere hyperbole; the castigated king is assimilated to another figure, whom the prophet's readers could recognize. A reference to Satan is unlikely,[18] and the idea that Ezekiel borrowed from a pagan myth lacks proper supporting evidence. He may have used, and dressed in his own manner, the same popular tradition which the writer of Genesis rewrote (so Dubarle 1967: 54 with n. 1), but a more economic solution (Occam's razor!) is that he freely fitted what he knew from Genesis into his poem, to suit his purpose –

---

[17] Ligier (1960: 264f.) thinks of Gn. 3:15 when he sees 'the serpent' mentioned in Am. 9:3 or the 'heels' in the case of women abused by barbarous soldiers (Je. 13:22); but this is too tenuous.

[18] Although the 'satanological' interpretations is widespread among evangelical Christians, it cannot be sustained. Any allusion which readers are to pick up 'between the lines' must be to something well known, and that was not the case for Satan at Ezekiel's stage of the history of revelation. The king of Tyre is to die as a *man* (v. 9), reduced to ashes on the ground (v. 18); nowhere else in Scripture is there any hint that Satan should be seen in that passage. Many have drawn the suggestion from the title 'cherub' (*k⁽e⁾rûb*) by which the king as addressed (vv. 14, 16), but (a) Satan is never called a cherub in the Bible; (b) with ancient versions, it is better to read here (without changing the Hebrew letters) 'You were . . . with a cherub' and 'a cherub expelled you'. Almost all modern commentators have abandoned the 'satanological' reading.

against the king of Tyre (Tidiman 1987: 66).[19] Like Adam in the
beginning, the king of Tyre was given dominion over the earth,
and favoured with the finest environment 'in the Garden of
God'; gold and onyx are mentioned in both passages (Ezk.
28:13; Gn. 2:11f.).[20] Like Adam, the king was created in a state
of perfection or integrity, with nothing to be ashamed of. Like
Adam, he coveted and claimed equality with the gods, through
both wisdom and the mastery of the ultimate secrets (Ezk. 28:2,
6, 17). Like Adam, he would suffer the loss of his paradise by
the agency of the $k^e r\hat{u}\underline{b}\hat{\imath}m$, whom I take as the symbol of the
most excellent forces of creation in the service of God (Ezk.
28:16; Gn. 3:24). Like Adam, he was sentenced to die as a
humbling reminder of his earthiness (Ezk. 28:9, 18) – 'You
Adam,' $'at\hat{a}$ $'\bar{a}\underline{d}\bar{a}m$, reads the apostrophe in verse 9. A resound-
ing echo indeed!

In the Writings category, some psalms also may allude to
Adam's punishment: 'They are not stricken with Adam' (Ps.
73:5, with the French *Bible de Jérusalem*); 'Indeed, you shall die as
Adam' (Ps. 82:7, as interpreted by Gordis 1957: 127 n. 16). The
wisdom books, however, are more likely to recall the Genesis
story, itself imbued with a sapiential spirit. The book of Proverbs
sees the emblem of wisdom in the tree of life (3:18; *cf.* 11:30 and
13:12). Although there is no reminiscence in the wording, the
final warning of the great oration on Wisdom's agency in
creation, Proverbs 8:36, closely agrees with the message of
Genesis 3. Job 31:33 was quoted by the older divines, who found
the reference to Genesis 3:12 'manifest' (Turretin 1847: 519
[VIII.3.8], *manifeste*): 'If I have concealed my sin as Adam did'
(NIV mg.). Dubarle (1967: 54) discerns a tradition of the first
man's usurpation of wisdom in Job 15:7f.: 'Were you born the
first Adam . . . did you grab for yourself wisdom?' And then
comes the most reflective of all biblical books: Ecclesiastes. As
already mentioned, according to recent interpreters, it 'is best
understood as an arresting but thoroughly orthodox exposition

---

[19] Critical datings of Gn. 2 – 3 (J) still assign to the writing of this narrative a
date much earlier than Ezekiel; hence the strong probability that Ezekiel was
familiar with the Genesis text.

[20] In the uncertain word of Ezk. 28:13 – *neqe\underline{b}*, translated 'mountings',
'engravings' or 'spangles' in the main modern versions – could there be an
allusion to the $n^e q\bar{e}\underline{b}\hat{a}$, 'female', of Gn. 1:27?

of Genesis 1 – 3' (Clemens 1994: 5).[21] Given the obvious allusion of Ecclesiastes 12:7 and 3:20 to Genesis 3:19, he continues,

> ... the remaining themes of these chapters [of Ecclesiastes] should be viewed within the conceptual framework of Genesis 1 – 3, related as they are to the dominant preoccupation with death. This assumption appears especially apposite for the prominent topics of toil, (thwarted) knowledge of good and evil, sin, and the positive recommendations to eat and embrace toil as God's assignment to humanity (p. 6).

Many verbal correspondences confirm this. The idea of the 'fall', the sequence of righteousness and perversion, is strongly expressed in 7:29: 'God made *hā'ādām* upright, but they have sought many schemes' – the presence of the article favours the collective understanding of *'ādām*, 'humankind', but a more individual reference is not absolutely ruled out. I cannot follow Clemens in seeing a Genesis allusion in the serpent of 10:8, 11, but the possibility of the typical woman of 7:26, 28 being Eve, and of the 'one sinner [who] spoils a lot of good' (9:18) being Adam, is more attractive (p. 7). On the basis of such possible hints we cannot attain certainty, but the cumulative force of plausibilities enables us to resist the pessimistic assessment of some regarding Old Testament echoes of the Genesis narrative of Eden.

If we search for echoes in the New Testament (apart from Rom. 5), our findings are more plentiful. In the synoptic gospels, as we saw, Jesus' retort to the Pharisees on marriage and divorce (Mt. 19:4–8 and par.) evidences an (implicit) creation–fall– redemption scheme. Something quite radical, which must account for people's hardness of hearts, happened after Genesis 1 – 2: 'In the beginning, it was not so.' The same tragic event produced the constant shedding of innocent blood since the murder of Abel (Mt. 23:35). Subtle exegesis finds the paradisiac theme in Mark's story of Jesus' temptation, which mentions wild

---

[21] Clemens builds upon the work of Charles C. Forman and Hans Wilhelm Hertzberg (p. 8 n. 8).

beasts resting peacefully with him.[22] The suggestion is that Jesus' victorious obedience in the wilderness symmetrically reverses Adam's defeat in the garden. Similarly, 'Luke's arrangement of Jesus' genealogy (Lk. 3:23–38; cf. Mt. 1:2–16) and its juxtaposition with the temptation narrative (Lk. 4:1–13 . . .) constitute an Adam–Christ typology'; 'unlike the first Son of God who fell when tempted by Satan . . . Jesus, the second Son of God, does not' (Evans 1992: 864). Luke 10:18f. associates Satan's downfall and the symbol of serpents trampled down, a likely reminder of the serpent's doom in Genesis 3:15.

The Johannine corpus shows a distinct interest in the 'original' (*archaios*), serpent of Eden, who is identified as the devil (Rev. 12:9; 20:2); this motif is combined with that of the dragon (the Leviathan of Is. 27:1). Jesus, in obvious reference to Genesis 3, insists that the devil was a liar and a murderer from (that) *archē* (Jn. 8:44). He recognizes the kin or seed of the serpent in the followers of lies and murderous thoughts.

Paul alludes to the fate of the serpent, soon to be crushed under the feet of the faithful, in Romans 16:20. He stresses the tempter's cunning, which effectively led Eve astray (2 Cor. 11:3; 1 Tim. 2:14).[23] The creation–fall pattern is very much on his mind when he comments on the subjection of all creatures to 'vanity', 'emptiness' or 'frustration', *not by their own choice* (Rom. 8:20) – a clear indication of Adam's responsibility. The same thought could be seen in the next clause, 'because of him who subjected it', for Paul's emphasis falls on the man's fault, and this would lead to a correspondence with Genesis 3:17, 'because of you'. Yet the participle 'he who subjected it', an exercise of sovereignty, is best taken as designating God himself, together with the following words, 'in hope' because of God. 'To vanity was the creation subjected, not by its own choice', for it was the sequel of Adam's transgression; however, because it was the God of grace and hope who intervened, 'the subjection was in hope . . .' Does a preceding passage, Romans 7:7–13, also build upon reminiscences of Genesis 2 – 3? Unlike

---

[22] So Graham H. Twelftree (1992: 825b), with a reference to Justin Martyr, *Dialogue with Trypho* 103. Robert H. Gundry (1993: 58f.) remains sceptical of the allusion, which, he argues, would have led to 'the wild beasts were with him', rather than 'he was with the wild beasts'.

[23] I do not accept that *(ex)apataō* has, of itself, any sexual connotation.

some interpreters,[24] I do not perceive any distinct connections; nowhere else does Paul suggest the presence of dormant sin *before* the moment when 'by one man sin entered into the world'.[25] Does the Christological 'hymn' of Philippians 2:6ff. implicitly contrast Jesus' humble obedience, which led to supreme lordship, with Adam's presumptuous disobedience, which brought him shame and bondage and death? This hypothesis (developed, *e.g.*, by Ligier 1961: 346ff.), is highly suggestive, but it lacks precise clues in the text. By contrast, the apostle's forceful elaboration of the Genesis passage is manifest in 1 Corinthians 15. To be sure, in verses 44ff., he does not distinguish between what belongs to Adam's 'earthiness' and what belongs to his moral-spiritual corruption, for he is interested in the new mode of bodily existence and intent on proving its superior glory. But the decisive statement in verse 56, 'the sting of death is sin' (death being 'the final enemy', v. 26), shows that what Adam fatally caused ('all die in Adam', v. 22) is bound to the *sin* he committed. It is a short and fully warranted step from 1 Corinthians 15:21, 'through a man death [came]', to Romans 5:12, 'through one man sin entered into the world, and, through sin, death . . .'

The weight of the evidence for which we have combed Old and New Testaments allows us to dispose of the negative view that the Romans 5 reference to the Eden story is an isolated bolt from the blue, of little significance.

The Eden story and literary discernment

Similarities do obtain between the Genesis narrative (Gn. 2 – 3)

---

[24] Grelot (1973: 17) goes so far as to call it *le nœud*, the knot. Garlington (1994: 113ff.) follows Dunn with a special note (118f.), on Paul, Adam and Eve; he makes the stimulating suggestion that Paul may not have distinguished formally between Adam and Eve as individuals.

[25] This argument is put forward by Gundry (1980: 230–232), who summarizes Lyonnet's case in favour of the Adamic reading of Rom. 7 and offers a refutation, pointing to the fact that the Gn. 3 prohibition was directed not at desiring but at eating, and pointing also to Paul's division of periods. Gundry's own interpretation, in which he refers Paul's language to his experience of puberty and of the bar mitzvah, fails to convince me that Paul speaks autobiographically in Rom. 7. Porter (1990a: 11; *cf.* 30) also judges that 'the most important point to be made is that Romans 7:7–25 does not appear to be a discussion of the origin of sin . . .'

and the myths of the nations; we need not deny them. But the dissimilarities are even more striking. Against the background of ancient lore, original features stand out boldly; the antithesis of the two trees, and indeed the presence of the tree of the knowledge of good and evil, are unique. This is no clumsy interpolation, but is structurally decisive, as each of the trees represents one of the two clauses of the creation covenant (Gn. 2:16f.) which held out either full freedom to eat and live or the certainty of death as the penalty of foolish transgression. The two trees signal that life and death are tied to human choice, a chief lesson of the story. If we compare the serpent's role with the verses in the *Epic of Gilgamesh* where a serpent steals the plant of life while the hero is taking a bath (IX, 287ff.), we find a marked contrast. Attempting a comparison borders on the ridiculous. More generally, the serpent figures in the two narratives are evaluated in contrasting ways; whereas the near-eastern serpent is a helpful deity, from whom humans can learn the magic secrets of health and fecundity, and how to penetrate the unknown future, the astute serpent of Genesis causes deception and death.[26] The whole atmosphere differs profoundly from that of myth. Gerhard von Rad (1963: 95) has sensed that the Genesis narrative 'has very little in common with a real myth'. Dubarle (1967: 51 n. 1) approvingly summarizes Martin Noth's opinion: 'The author of chapters 2 – 3 has not followed any of the ancient Near East creation narratives, but has simply used detailed images to express what was his own creation.' Other critical scholars warn against too hasty a categorization of the account as 'myth'.[27]

'Just as one swallow does not make a summer,' Gibert (1986: 97) wisely remarks, 'a few mythical traits do not constitute a mythical story.' It was Dubarle's well argued thesis (in 1958, at least) that figurative language drawn from myths may perfectly

[26] *Cf.* the fine appreciation of this point in Derousseaux 1975: 15.
[27] Derousseaux (1975: 9) concludes: 'the narration of Genesis is not a myth strictly speaking'; if one adopts Malinowski's definition, 'our account is not a myth' (p. 20). Pierre Gibert (1986: 92) first quotes Jean-Pierre Vernant on the methodological danger of applying such an elusive and equivocal notion as that of myth, and then, observing differences with what M. Eliade calls myth, he asks: 'Actually, are we meeting here a myth and the spirit of myth?' (p. 97), and suggests that our passage shows that Israel carried out a real *démythisation* (p. 99).

well suit an essentially historical revelation (1967: 51 [with n. 2]
–55).[28] Such a combination of imagery (of whatever provenance) and a message about definite events is familiar in
Scripture; one need only think of Ezekiel's allegories, of
apocalyptic visions, and of many of Jesus' parables. It involves
no tension. It should cause no embarrassment. Thinking
otherwise is unwarranted prejudice, which many liberals share
with nervous, 'right-wing', orthodox commentators. The real
issue when we try to interpret Genesis 2 – 3 is not whether we
have a historical account of the fall, but whether or not we may
read it as the account of a historical fall. The problem is not
historiography as a genre narrowly defined – in annals,
chronicles, or even saga – but correspondence with discrete
realities in our ordinary space and sequential time.

Understanding the parabolic dress of the literary (or
rhetorical) medium used also disposes of Ricœur's most telling
argument, an argument which centres on the 'lapse of time' in
the story (1967: 252ff.). He argues that the 'fall' does not occur
at a given point of time, but is spread over several moments; did
not sin enter the world when Eve began to believe the serpent's
lie, and, clearly, when desire for the fruit overcame her respect
for God's command? But, if this is so, why were her eyes not
opened immediately? If the transition from innocence to sin
were one of total discontinuity, it would have been instanta-
neous. Since it is not so in Genesis 3, we may conclude, so
Ricœur reasons, that the tale is not interested in chronological
sequence, but only in the ideal scheme of disobedience; it is a
myth.

We could reply that the true human present – 'saddle-
shaped', as William James is reported to have said[29] – can never
be reduced to an abstract mathematical point (maybe Kierkegaard's 'instant' is untrue because it misses this concrete

---

[28] Dubarle (1967: 51 n. 1) mentions Albin van Hoonacker (1918: 373–400).
This major pioneer in Roman Catholic biblical studies valiantly defends the
basic historicity of Gn. 2 – 3. He offers a refutation of the views of Gunkel,
Albert and Wellhausen, and lucidly recognizes, at the end, the part played by
one's conviction on the status ('inspired' or otherwise) of the text.

[29] 'For, as William James expressed it, the specious present is a "saddle-back",
not a "knife-edge". It contains something of the "no longer" and something of
the "not yet" in an experience which, nevertheless, is a unitary present' (Rule
1955: 1116a).

extension). We live by 'grains' of time of a certain thickness and consistency, not by infinitely small divisions of the millisecond. In Scripture, the 'unit' of human time seems to be the day: 'the day you eat . . .' The lapse of time in Genesis 3 does not destroy the unity of the event; it testifies to its human character. But in reply to Ricœur's comments we can also say that the sacred writer's intention, as shown by the literary device he chose, is not to reveal the particular *modus accidendi* of the first sin in the precise way in which it happened then. The peculiar circumstances would have had anecdotal significance, of little profit to us. The historical break away from God's fellowship is told parabolically so that its universal import may be evident for our discernment and admonition.

Kierkegaard's (1980: 32) reflection on the same feature of our text is worth pondering. As the Genesis narrative reads, he observes, 'sin came into the world by a sin'. In other words, sin presupposes itself; when one looks for a root or cause of the sinful act, Eve's desire before the concrete violation of the command must itself be categorized as sin.[30] The biblical story profoundly shows that sin's entrance can only mean a qualitative leap – much to the dislike of reason, which has invented instead a myth, and has read it into Genesis 3. Kierkegaard appears to be a better guide than most Kierkegaardians.

Is the import of Adam's name 'generic'? Of course! What a discovery for modern scholarship! It has been the very soul of the traditional doctrine of original sin that Adam the individual was at the same time humankind; to consider him as a private character acting in a private capacity would be a complete misreading of both text and tradition. Orthodox interpreters may readily welcome Kant's oft-quoted admonition, *Mutato nomine, de te fabula narratur.*[31] The same applies to aetiological purpose.

The issue is whether Adam's historic individuality conflicts with a representative role. The concept of 'headship' exactly combines the two. That Adam as 'head' is the race 'in person' involves no clear contradiction or obvious misuse of logic.

---

[30] Kierkegaard (1980: 40f.) lucidly criticizes attempts to make *concupiscentia* less than sinful.

[31] 'By a different name, about you the tale is told'; quoted *e.g.* by Hughes 1989: 110f., Kant himself having borrowed the phrase from Horace, *Satires* i.1.

Exegetically, Richard Hess (1990) has shown in a fine study that the use of the name '*āḏām* moves from the generic sense in Genesis 1 to referential service as a personal name in Genesis 4:25, while in between it functions as the *title* for the male individual who is in charge of the Garden. In Genesis 2:4b – 3:24,

> . . . it is appropriate that the references to '*dm* . . . be to a particular individual. However, as it intends to explain or teach concerning the present status of humanity in relation to God and the world, it is appropriate that the usage of '*dm* be more general than a personal name, *i.e.* that it be potentially capable of application to all humanity. A title, such as 'The Man', suits these requirements (p. 12).

We may, therefore, confidently discard the *a priori* rejection of the church dogma based on the meaning of Adam as 'Man' (that is, 'Human Being').

Able thinkers, however, have had misgivings about Adam's individual existence (and the 'headship' structure will be discussed later in this exploratory work). Bernard Ramm (1985) does not wholly dispel the ambiguity; he repeatedly stresses the 'generic' meaning as if he were uneasy with a clear historical interpretation, but he never denies that interpretation outright, and even seems to express some degree of adherence to it.[32] Kierkegaard is commonly credited with a denial of the 'historic view' of Genesis 2 – 3,[33] but we should not under-

---

[32] See Ramm 1985: 69ff. for his emphasis on the generic character: 'the generic or type is more important than the person' (p. 70); 'Adam is a generic man, Eve is the generic woman, and the sin is a generic sin' (p. 71); as he extols 'theology by narration', he defines the exercise in such a way ('theology is being expressed by telling a story', p. 69) as to give rise to fears that history becomes mere form by which to express concepts. But Ramm disowns that thought: 'the human race went astray as a race at its headwaters. The Fall is a historical event' (p. 81); Adam is to be read 'as both a generic figure and the person' (p. 72, *cf.* 75). Curiously, he affirms that 'generic history' *represents* actual history, but indirectly: 'The two events correspond, but certainly not in a one-on-one, factual sense' (p. 83). Strimple (1987: 143–152) voices deep concerns and strong criticisms (referring favourably to my *In the Beginning*).

[33] Ramm (1985: 135) writes: 'In Kierkegaard's thought Gen. 3 is not about a historical event but is rather the existential cross-section of the act of sin.

estimate the subtlety of his position. Certainly, he sharply criticizes traditional Augustinian doctrine: 'Adam is placed fantastically outside history. Adam's sin is then more than something past [*plus quam perfectum*]' (1980: 26). He is intent on making each individual 'the Adam of [his or her] own soul', to recall *2 Baruch*'s famous phrase: 'At every moment, the individual is both himself and the race' (54:10; p. 28);[34] and sin happens only through that individual's decision, just as in Adam's case (pp. 35, 60). Yet he does distinguish Adam from the rest of humankind as he speaks repeatedly of a 'quantitative' difference, and he can write: 'Hereditary sin is something present, it is sinfulness, *and Adam is the only one in whom it was not found,* since it came into being through him' (p. 26, my italics). He adds: 'In the foregoing, it has been said several times that the view presented in this work does not deny the propagation of sinfulness through generation, or, in other words, that sinfulness has its history through generation' (p. 47). Part of the complexity is tied to the shade of meaning of the 'sinfulness' from which 'sin' arises, while 'expressed precisely and accurately, sinfulness is in the world only insofar as it comes into the world by sin' (p. 33).[35] Whatever the Dane's exact thought, his reluctance to let go entirely of a primeval element, seen in a historical sequence, deserves notice.

Karl Barth's ambiguity has still other parameters. If Adam is for him the *Überschrift,* the label or title over the whole of human history and all its meaning and meaninglessness (1956: 507f.), his concern is less to blur Adam's historical individuality than to make him thoroughly subordinate, as to role and

---

Therefore it is the diagnosis of every person's fall from God into sin.' *Cf.* pp. 53f., 77.

[34] But see Kierkegaard 1980: 231 n. 13: according to G. Malantschuk, the unity of individual and race is the historical task, starting from the contradiction between them.

[35] Since Adam, he continues, 'sensuousness is constantly degraded to mean sinfulness' (p. 58, *cf.* 63); 'the moment sin is posited, temporality is sinfulness' (p. 92). Probably in order to ease the sinfulness/sin relationship, the French translators Knud Ferlov and Jean-J. Gateau have used the word *peccabilité,* which suggests merely the possibility of sinning (*Le Concept de l'angoisse,* Paris: Gallimard, 1935). But both English translations (Thomte's, and also Walter Lowrie's *The Concept of Dread*; Princeton: Princeton University Press, 1944) have chosen 'sinfulness', which seems the nearest equivalent to Kierkegaard's term.

significance, to the true First Adam, Jesus Christ (pp. 512f.).
His concept of 'saga', while making irrelevant all comparison
with palaeontology, does not exclude historical existence. But
'there never was a golden age. There is no point in looking
back to one. The first man was immediately the first sinner' (p.
508). Dogmatic interest, here, weighs heavily upon biblical
interpretation.

None of the textual features I have reviewed prevents or
renders improbable a historical reading. Positively, two considerations tend to show that such a reading, with due
allowances for genre and mode of expression, is actually
required, thus providing an Old Testament basis for the New
Testament use of the passage. First, Genesis 2 – 3 stands as 'item
1' of a grand genealogical series; it belongs, as the first link in
the chain, to the structure of the Genesis *tôlᵉḏôṯ* (genealogy).
Adam appears as a patriarch among the other patriarchs, in the
sequence of ordinary time. Dubarle (1975: 53) had rightly
observed that Genesis

> . . . gathers and organises the traditional accounts of
> origins and it creates an imperceptible continuity
> between them and memoirs that are properly speaking
> historical. Amongst the other peoples of the ancient
> world, myths did not undergo a similar treatment.

He had, secondly, noticed the mention of the first couple's
descendants in Genesis 3:15 and 20 (p. 58). Derousseaux (1975:
22) described these chapters 'as a porchway to the great history
of salvation that goes from Abraham to the Davidic dynasty' and
could write of a 'foundational event that eludes the hold of
history and is yet found in history'.[36] Gibert makes the most of
the argument. He highlights three characteristics of history as
opposed to legend and myth: chronological continuity in a
sequence of causes and effects; characters appearing as
responsible agents; and a 'judicial' activity on the historian's
part, showing a sense of the complexity of human behaviour. 'In
the story of Adam and Eve, paradoxical as it may seem, these

---

[36] Derousseaux mentions 'the first choice of the ancestor' as the source of
corruption, but he encourages ambiguity as he adds: 'The writer of Gen. 2 – 3
does not think of an original "fall".'

three ingredients of historical narratives can be found . . .'
(1986: 10; *cf.* 115).

Corresponding to Gilbert's second characteristic, the emphasis on responsibility, the most striking textual datum could be the structure of the canon's introductory section. There is not one table of origins, but two. The first (Gn. 1:1 – 2:3) is on the origin of being, the second (Gn. 2:4 – 3:24) on the origin of evil. Hermeneutical myopia sees two parallel, virtually rival, creation accounts – a clumsy arrangement indeed. But Umberto Cassuto (1961: 92) had already discerned that the precise lesson the Torah wishes to convey 'flows from the continuity of the two sections'. All the ills that plague human existence – shame, strife, pain, toil, death – stem from human disobedience. In the absolute beginning, it was not so; it was 'superlatively good' (Gn. 1:31). Derousseaux (1975: 23) has perceived the contrast with the myths of the heathen. In the famous Babylonian epic *Enuma eliš*, for instance, man is made of clay and of the blood of a fallen god, Kingu. Hence,

> . . . Man is not, at birth, an innocent and pure being. A divine blood, to be sure, flows in his veins, but of a guilty and reprobate god. It is a polluted blood, that carries sin and death. Ultimately, man bears the penalty of a sin he has not committed. They, the gods, have unleashed the Sin-Death pair . . . Through the gods evil entered into the world.[37]

Ricœur has recognized the purpose of Genesis with unsurpassed clarity: 'The aetiological myth of Adam [as he still calls it] is the most extreme attempt to separate the origin of evil from the origin of the good; its intention is to set up a *radical* origin of evil distinct from the more *primordial* origin of the goodness of things' (1967: 233). He has observed the solidarity of this original feature with the prophetic denunciation of sin and with the themes of Yahweh's holiness and of his rule through his Word (p. 240).[38] And it means *history*:

---

[37] P. Garelli and M. Leibovici, *La Naissance du monde*, Sources orientales 1 (Paris: Seuil, 1959), p. 127, as quoted by Derousseaux 1975: 7.

[38] *Cf.* p. 243: the 'twofold confession', which corresponds to Gn. 1 and 2 – 3, 'is the very essence of repentance'.

> History too, then, is an original dimension and not a 're-enactment' of the drama of creation. It is History, not Creation, that is a Drama. Thus Evil and History are contemporaneous; neither Evil nor History can any longer be referred to some primordial disorder; *Evil becomes scandalous at the same time as it becomes historical* (p. 203, my italics).

In spite of Ricœur's other positions, such a witness is enough to show that an essentially historical reading of Genesis 2 – 3 does not impose an alien viewpoint upon the text. The burden of proof, I suggest, rests with those who depart from it and treat the Eden narrative as an 'omni-temporal' myth.

The Eden story and theological reflection

Other thinkers have reflected on the historical bent of the Genesis account, and have approached Ricœur's lucidity. Emil Brunner perceived that erasing the distinction between humanity as created and humanity as sinful would shatter the foundations. He could even add, 'When we realize how much is at stake, we can at least understand the contortions of Fundamentalist theology, which, in themselves, are most unfortunate' (1952: 51).[39] More recently, Adolphe Gesché, of Louvain, has sensed how concerned the Bible is to point to the radical strangeness of evil: 'Manifestly, for one who reads the narratives of Genesis, God does not include evil in a rational coherence' (1993: 33);[40] it cannot be explained and comprehended as an aspect, element or entailment of the metaphysical fabric of our existence.

We cannot be too radical here. The perfect goodness of God's creation rules out the tiniest root, seed or germ of evil. This is why I would not endorse C. S. Lewis's risky formulation, which he ventured with extreme caution; he wrote of the 'weak spot' in creation and in human nature: 'The self-surrender which [humankind] practised before the Fall meant no struggle but

---

[39] He goes on: 'Over against a theory of Evolution which sweeps away all ideas of Creation and Sin, Fundamentalism, in spite of its curious aberrations of thought, is absolutely right.'

[40] 'Dieu ne se fait aucune raison du mal.' *Cf.* pp. 104ff.

only the delicious overcoming of an infinitesimal self-adherence which delighted to be overcome . . .' (1940: 69). Rather, I would follow the Kierkegaardian either/or: *either* there was no struggle at all, but unmixed and blissful obedience (we should not slander creation by speaking of a 'weak spot' in its framework, and think we have found a partial explanation of the fall); *or* human beings as created did adhere to self in a way that contradicted their divine calling, and were not created perfectly good (maybe they did get a drop of Kingu's blood in their veins!).

This is why I would even question the usual way of speaking of sin's *possibility* in Eden. On the surface, nothing could be more obvious; since it happened, it must previously have been possible. But is the application of this logic justified? Actually, it presupposes a continuity, a homogeneous field of virtualities and actualities (such a field as we rightly take for granted in our experience of the world, on the basis of creation), whereas applying the logic to the first intrusion of sin involves a subtle, hidden denial of the *discontinuity* of sin, that is, of its radical strangeness. Certainly, sin was not impossible; the human being was not immutable. In that sense, one could speak of a merely theoretical possibility of sin. But a *real* possibility, to borrow Kierkegaard's significant phrase (1980: 23),[41] some weakness worth mentioning in the description of our created nature, would mean a germ of evil, a crack in the divine Potter's handiwork.[42] We must reject the thought, despite the charge of subtlety and paradox.

My suspicion regarding the abuse of 'possibility' makes me wary of following the traditional (Augustinian) analysis of the assistance of God's grace in Paradise. Turretin, as a classical representative of that doctrine, explains that Adam was given the *auxilium sine quo non*, the divine help without which it is impossible to obey God, but not the *auxilium quo*, which is the efficacious help leading to actual obedience (1847: 550 [IX.7.7]). But the first help meant mere possibility for him, a possibility which never comes to fruition if the second help is

---

[41] *Cf.* pp. 41ff. and 61 for his descriptions of anxiety, in innocence, as the possibility.

[42] Barth (1956: 409f.) also rejected the idea of a prior 'possibility' of sin, as he rightly saw that this slippery notion leads to excuses for sin.

not added! Pascal, in the *Lettres provinciales*, showed the Jesuits that the chief characteristic of what they called 'sufficient grace' was that it was not sufficient. Presumably, unsatisfactory exercises of the theological mind, such as these, are produced by the attempt to *comprehend* evil or sin; that is, to find a place for it within a rational whole. As radical strangeness, alienation, disorder, however, it is *atopos*, placeless. Kierkegaard (1980: 14) also noted that sin has no place *and is defined by that trait*.[43]

Whatever one's preference on this most important yet fine point of philosophical theology,[44] the key question for the present study is this: may we follow Brunner and Ricœur and value the meaning while discarding the event? Their statement of the significance of the Genesis sequence, whereby evil is introduced *after* creation, is coupled with an equally vocal rejection of that same sequence as having really occurred in time and space. The question cannot be avoided: is it responsible theology to retain and enjoy the 'profit' of a historical understanding of sin without 'paying the price'?

Since Immanuel Kant, modern theology has often tried to extol the meaning for faith of the great events of the gospel while denying their factual base in the name of rational criticism. That treatment has been applied to the Easter message by countless preachers and interpreters. I submit that presumptions, at least, are against such a disjunction. It seems to lead to an 'as if' theology, an 'as if' Christianity. Actually, Ricœur quotes from Kant on the origin of sin: 'every such [evil] action must be regarded *as though* the individual had fallen into it directly from a state of innocence', and he comments: 'Everything is in this "as if".'[45] As if good news? Is it possible to dehistoricize a message built on the testimony that these events happened? One remembers the man who thought that birds

[43] This chapter has been constantly shifting, in its quotations, from Kierkegaard as an opponent to Kierkegaard as an ally. I find in his work two conflicting tendencies: he wishes to safeguard the 'qualitative leap', the discontinuity of sin (with which I agree), but he also explains sin 'psychologically' as arising out of anxiety, which has a metaphysical character. Gesché (1993: 105 n. 6) perceives the contrast with dualism (which gives evil a symmetrical place); he refers to Kant, but I doubt his interpretation.

[44] I wonder, for instance, whether this divergence on 'possibility' lies at the root of the divergence between Eberhard Jüngel's thought and mine; see Jüngel 1977: 291ff.

[45] Ricœur 1974a: 435, quoting from Kant 1960: 36 (my italics).

and planes would fly more easily in a vacuum – and the teachers who retain the form of godliness, but deny what gives it its strength (2 Tim. 3:5). Robert Spaemann (1991: 49) wisely affirms that 'The Christian religion can never be severed from some (at least) factual truths', and 'the tendency to keep their number as low as possible, in order to avoid conflicts, involves high costs'.[46]

Do advocates of meaning without definite fact, when they deal with 'originating' original sin, clearly show *how* they can so proceed? When the sequence of righteousness and sinfulness is denied, on what basis do they keep the latter distinct from the metaphysical formula of human nature? Is that distinction credible? Brunner's fall 'is no more an empirical event than the Creation; it lies behind or above the empirical plane' (1947: 399); 'the Creation and the Fall both lie behind the historical visible actuality, as their presuppositions which are always present . . .' (p. 142). How can such a concept be clarified and justified? And if 'the fatality of the Fall consists . . . in the fact that every human being, in his own person, and in union with the rest of humanity, every day renews this Fall afresh, and cannot help doing so' (p. 172), should not the conclusion be that it is literal 'fatality', a feature of being? Are we far from Greek tragedy, which makes man's guilt his fate (p. 193)? Nearer to Kant's inspiration, Reinhold Niebuhr's emphasis on 'responsibility despite inevitability' (1941: 255ff.), and Ricœur's on the rational symbol of the power of evil 'already there' in our experience of freedom (1974c: 282f.; 1974b: 305, and *passim*), offer little more than words in praise of paradox to offset the greater likelihood of the metaphysical interpretation. That interpretation leads to the conclusion that humans are evil 'as if' they had fallen; but if they did not *really* fall, they must *be* evil from creation and by creation.[47]

To his credit, we must note N. P. Williams's clear-headed

---

[46] My translation 'factual truths' renders his *vérités de fait* (in French in Spaemann's German text) and *Tatsachenwahrheiten*.

[47] I put the same objection to Pannenberg (1994), whose treatment is finer than most. He clearly discerns why the Augustinian solution has recourse to Adam: in order to combine both guilt and structural universality (p. 253). But he thinks he has no such need: 'Our voluntary committing of it [sin] is enough to make us guilty. There does not have to be a primal and once-for-all event of a fall for which Adam was guilty quite apart from all entanglement in sin'; 'Adam

sensitivity to the requirement for historicity. Before he starts speculating on the 'race-soul' and 'Life-Force of the universe', he shrewdly criticizes Kant's noumenal, and therefore timeless, fall:

> The conception of a 'timeless act' is one which seems to involve a contradiction in terms . . . For it would seem that an act of the will necessarily implies change, if not in the external world, at least in the agent; it at least involves the idea of a transition on the part of the agent from a previous condition, either of inertia or of differently directed activity; and a transition is a change, and change involves time (1927: 501, 505).[48]

Against Tennant, he observes that the evolutionistic suppression of the fall, together with the affirmation of the 'empirical inevitability' of sin, 'betrays [God] into actual sin' (p. 532). More recently, Christoph Schönborn (1991b: 75–78, 93) also upholds Adam's historicity as a foundational truth.[49] Mere denial that it matters may not pass as evidence.[50]

Scrutiny of the work of those thinkers who retain the meaning

---

was simply the first sinner', whose behaviour we repeat (p. 263). Pannenberg's solution seems to be that our created self-centredness, which is not bad in itself (pp. 250, 260), very easily slides into self-fixation at any cost, which is sinful and manifests itself basically in anxiety and excessive desire (pp. 250, 261): 'the perversion of the relation of the finitude of the self to the Infinite and Absolute is so close that except in the case of express distinction of the self in its finitude from God, the self does in fact become the infinite basis and reference point for all objects, thus usurping the place of God'; 'to that extent sin is bound up with the natural conditions of human existence' (p. 261). This confers a metaphysical tinge on the universal spread of sin (for which Pannenberg compensates by driving a wedge between sin and guilt, p. 261, and introducing a measure of optimism, p. 275). This is tied to his strong affirmation of creaturely independence, which should not degenerate, however, into 'autonomy' (pp. 264f.).

[48] Williams chides Hegel's view for confusing creation and the fall, and thus transforming Christianity into some sort of Gnosticism.

[49] I was led to Schönborn's work by Vanneste 1994: 376, who rejects Schönborn's position, and takes refuge in paradox (p. 378).

[50] Many Roman Catholic scholars have been attracted by a compromise solution: 'a primal sin collective: a murder of which a whole group would have been guilty (Mgr Philips), an idolatrous act perpetrated by many people (Cardinal Daniélou)' (Delhaye 1975: v n. 7). Josef Scharbert (1968: 112f.) adopts a similar position. Others, going further, do away with any single catastrophe, but still retain the idea of historical beginning; originating original

of the fall but let go the fact bears out my thesis. In spite of their lucid perception, they are unable to preserve the benefits of historicity untarnished. A 'metaphysical' understanding of sin or evil filters into their views. The inevitability of sin in Brunner's or Niebuhr's perspective goes back to a hidden dualism of nature and freedom, the fundamental motif of their thinking. The 'real possibility' of sin before sin, located in anxiety, is bound up with what Kierkegaard (1980: 69) calls 'the prodigious *Widerspruch* [contradiction] that the immortal spirit is determined as *genus*'. Ricœur's case offers the most instructive illustration. After contrasting the intention of the Genesis story and the tragic myth (evil ultimately rooted in the divine), he considers that 'the tragic is *invincible*...' (1967: 327; *cf*. 323, 326, 346). The foil of Adam is the serpent, and Ricœur interprets this figure as representing the residue of the tragic experience of the world – the cosmic structure which invites us to treason (pp. 257f., *cf*. 234). Though anti-tragic, the Adamic 'myth' reaffirms something of tragic man and even of tragic god (p. 311). This is also the message of Job.[51] Only thus are we to escape the 'flatness' of ethical monotheism: 'Perhaps it is necessary also to envelop in darkness the divine . . .' (1974b: 309). The rational optimism which often follows metaphysical interpretations of evil (in spite of tragedy) also shows through occasionally:

> We sense that evil itself is part of the economy of superabundance . . . We must therefore have the courage to incorporate evil into the epic of hope. In a way that we know not, evil itself cooperates, works toward, the advancement of the Kingdom of God . . . Faith justifies the man of the *Aufklärung* [Enlightenment], for whom, in the great romance of culture, evil is a factor in the education of the human race, rather than the puritan, who never succeeds in taking the step from condemnation to mercy . . . (1974a: 439).

---

sin becomes the sum and nexus of many unfortunate inaugural choices, across generations, which constitute a sinful inheritance in racial-social solidarity. This appears to be the position of Dubarle (1967: 192ff., a 1967 addition) and Guilluy (1975: 176, 180, 191).

[51] Job 'is ready to identify his freedom with inimical necessity; he is ready to convert freedom and necessity into fate' (p. 321).

I do not recognize here the God in whose light (he *is* light) there is no darkness at all (1 Jn. 1:5), or the biblical horror at and hatred for evil (Rom. 12:9).

If evil is 'invincible' as a dimension of being, and yet a factor in our progress, should we conclude that it will never be defeated and 'cast out'? Although Ricœur does not say so, it seems a logical conclusion to draw. Only historical (and thus responsible) evil may be vanquished and perfectly eliminated. Historical evil, sin, the foe of both God and humankind, and true hope – to be distinguished from dialectical reversals – go together. Only if the problem is historical will the solution *happen.*

Maybe the link between the two human 'heads' of Romans 5 is stronger and more essential than many have thought.

Chapter Three

Discerning Paul's mind on Adam's role

Romans 5:12ff. fully deserves the appellation *sedes doctrinae*, the 'seat' or 'fundament' of the doctrine of original sin. Whenever this doctrine is discussed, Romans 5 is in the eye of the storm. The time has come for us to scrutinize the central text.

This seat is not very comfortable! Peter himself warned that his colleague Paul's letters contain passages difficult to understand (2 Pet. 3:16). In this controversial one, Romans 5, several formal features may afford some excuse to discomfited interpreters. The apostle's manner of dictating, so quick and elliptical at times, results here in a broken construction, an anacoluthon. The introductory 'just as', *hōsper*, in verse 12, is not matched by the corresponding 'so also' which one would have expected;[1] the argument in verse 13 branches off to explain a particular point, and Paul does not complete the structure after verse 14; the 'just as . . . so also' pattern appears, full-blown, only in verses 18–21. This involves parallelism, in order to bring out the correspondence between the one man Adam (and his disobedience) and the one man Jesus Christ (and his obedience). Here also a formal difficulty arises; the apostle insists on difference, lack of correspondence, between Adam and Christ. He expressly negates the 'as . . . so' scheme in verse 15a; 'it is not the case', he says. If this means that we should not expect perfect symmetry between the two parallel stories, how much should we expect?

Some copyists were disconcerted by the emphatic statement that people after Adam did not sin in the way he had done (v. 14; a few manuscripts omit the negative particle in 'those who had not sinned . . .'). It is understandable that they were tempted to 'correct' (mistakenly) the wording of the verse,

---

[1] 'Thus', *kai houtōs*, in v. 12c, cannot pass for the corresponding phrase, which ought to be *houtōs kai*, as Cranfield (1975: I, 272 n. 5) establishes.

since contemporary thinking on Adam's role, as we have seen, focused on Adam's setting a pattern and transmitting a bent that caused his descendants to sin like him. Paul's negation surprised them, and it surprises us. The proposition in verse 20a, 'the law was introduced (intervened) to multiply the offence', also strikes both ancient and modern readers as a paradox. Theologians and exegetes, then, should not incur too severe a reprimand if they grope somewhat awkwardly for Paul's mind in Romans 5 (and indeed I myself beg for charity on the part of the reader).

To simplify the task, we may immediately put aside those interpretations which project into the apostle's reasoning a modern, or maybe Gnostic, reading of Genesis 3 which is assimilated to timeless myth or to a symbol of omnitemporal human experience. Whatever one's critical conclusion on the genre of the primal story, Paul must be seen in his own context, and the scheme he outlines bears a strongly historical stamp. He is interested in the distinction of epochs. He repeatedly sets the one Adam over against the many human beings. Professor James Dunn's clear-cut judgment can hardly be gainsaid: 'What comes to expression here is not some concept of "corporate personality" or cosmic Man or theology of Adam as Everyman' (1988: 273).[2] Dunn rightly chides Cranfield for yielding to Barthian influence; his 'stretching of *typos* to include every man as a human being [Cranfield 1975: 295] distorts the typology unacceptably' (p. 277).[3] We may be certain that Paul, in Romans 5, attributed a major role to an individual Adam and to his transgression in the beginning; this is what he meant, regardless of whether it appeals to our sensitivities.

Interpreters who would not disown this preliminary stage of the argument are wont to follow one of two paths. They tend either to loosen the link between Adam and Christ or to tighten it; either they make the symmetry vague and flexible or they see it as stiff and strict. The first category, of course, leans towards Pelagius' position, and the second towards Augustine's. This chapter will try to assess the strengths and weaknesses of both

---

[2] Johnson (1974: 301 n. 20) also maintains that Paul regards Gn. 2 – 3 as historical, and Garlington (1994: 84) affirms 'that he *is* concerned with origins'.

[3] Dunn adds: 'Barth's insistence that not Adam but Jesus Christ is first . . . actually depends on a Gnostic Christology . . .'

approaches, albeit in cursory fashion. It happens that my own mind is uneasy with both of them, and so, with some trepidation, I shall put forward a new possibility for consideration.

Looser interpretations of Romans 5

Major commentaries such as those of Cranfield and Dunn acknowledge Adam's importance for Paul, yet they resist drawing too close a parallel with Christ's role in salvation. They suppose the key thought in the apostle's mind to be Adam's causality as the fountainhead of corruption. Adam introduced into the human world a propensity which produces sinning in his descendants' lives, and therefore brings death as a consequence of sin. This is the way the 'many' were made or constituted sinners (v. 19): all people die because all have sinned (throughout history, in their own individual lives); all have sinned because they were born with a bent towards sin; they were so born because Adam sinned first. Or, in Cranfield's words:

> We may assume that by the former statement Paul means that all other men (Jesus alone excepted) were constituted sinners through Adam's misdeed in the sense that, sin having once obtained entry into human life through it, they all in their turns lived sinful lives (1975: I, 290f.).

The clause in verse 12d, 'because all have sinned', is given the same meaning as in Romans 3:23; many consider this to be the 'natural' sense. In favour of that common interpretation, the witness of Jewish thinking in the first century AD is invoked (p. 280): Adam (or Eve, or the serpent) is viewed as the one who introduces universal death and as the source of the evil inclination (*yēṣer*). At the same time, there is an attempt to maintain individual responsibility. Sometimes the emphasis falls on the latter, as in *2 Baruch* (54:15, 19) – perhaps the Hillelite line; sometimes, perhaps under Shammaite inspiration, the doctrine shows a more deterministic cast, as in *4 Ezra* or at Qumran. The tension remains. Paul's theology, we are told, does not escape being pulled in these two directions: 'The primary causality for [humanity's] sinful and mortal condition is ascribed to [Adam], but a secondary resultant causality is attributed to the sinful conduct of all human beings.'[4]

Why, then, does the apostle emphasize Adam's causality? Cranfield (1975: I, 281) confidently answers: 'The purpose of the comparison is to make clear the universal range of what Christ has done.'[5] Dunn (1988: 273) notices that Paul's 'theme is original *death* more than original *sin*': he wishes to emphasize the universal rule of death. The cosmic scope harmonizes with the later allusion to the fall in Romans 8; it is also characteristic of the other Pauline development of the theme in 1 Corinthians 15: in Adam all die, in Christ all come back to life.

Such a reading deserves our consideration, for those who are aware of the elasticity of language, and the conditions under which all exegesis is obliged to labour, may hardly rule it out as impossible.[6] Yet difficulties spring to mind. It is rather strange that the core idea, or the hinge of the apostle's purported logic – that Adam communicated the sinful bent to his posterity – should not be expressed at all in the passage.[7] It *might* be implicit; undoubtedly, Paul did share the opinion; yet how surprising that he should not include something here, of all places, to make it clear! When Ramm (1985: 56) comments that 'sin is not seen so much as a formal breaking of a specified law but as a contagious disease that spreads through a population', I confess to some amazement; the quotation testifies to the ability of fine scholars to read into the text what they think should be there. Although his own reading of the text steers clear of

---

[4] This is how Fitzmyer (1993: 339) summarizes Paul's meaning; *cf.* Dunn 1988: 274.

[5] *Cf.* his phrase 'universal effectiveness', p. 283.

[6] In the main, it is Calvin's interpretation; yet I would hesitate to summarize his view as neatly as Johnson (1974: 307) does: 'he [Calvin] explicitly says we are not guilty of Adam's sin'. Calvin's French original of the passage cited (*Institutes* II.i.8) is slightly ambiguous. He says we are not condemned for another's fault *seulement* ('only'); we are not *seulement* under the judicial obligation, as if we had no sin ourselves; infants are condemned not *simplement* ('simply') for another's sin.

[7] Douglas J. Moo (1991: 337) observes shrewdly that all interpretations (including Luther's and Calvin's on the Augustinian side) that rely on the thought of inherited tendencies to sin as to the middle term between Adam's disobedience and death upon all have 'to supply the crucial "middle term" in the argument, Adam's having and passing on a corrupt nature'.

acknowledging judicial categories, Don Garlington (1994: 86) acknowledges that

> Vis-à-vis Cranfield and others, Ridderbos and Ber-
> kouwer are quite right that the present context directly
> concerns man's immediate involvement in Adam's sin
> and death, not moral corruption as such. This is why I
> have sought to emphasize that 'sin' in the first instance
> is not so much 'depravity' as a (damnation-)historical
> state introduced by Adam.

Paul's emphasis in Romans 5:18ff. on the *one* act of disobedience, which constituted all human beings sinners, is so insistent that the idea of Adam simply as the remote cause of sin's introduction fails to match the force of Paul's language. Apart from the disputed clause in verse 12, 'because all have sinned', nowhere does the apostle put forward the actual sinful tendencies or behaviour of humankind as the ground for their condemnation. As Johnson (1974: 310) writes, 'the silence is almost deafening'. Nor does the scheme that focuses on universal corruption fit with the unique phrase of verse 14, describing Adam as a *type* of the One who was coming. According to the looser reading, Adam's role is very different from Christ's in justification (for Christ does not justify his own by transmitting to them a 'good inclination'). Older Roman Catholic doctrine could accommodate a parallel here which heirs of the Reformation will denounce vehemently.[8] To reply that Paul stresses the *dis*similarity of Adam and Christ in verses

---

[8] Not all such heirs, however, retain their attachment to the *articulus stantis et cadentis ecclesiae* (the article [of faith] by which the church stands or falls, *i.e.* the doctrine of justification by faith) as understood by the Reformers, especially those influenced by the 'new view of Paul'. I have been surprised to read, from Garlington's pen (1994: 104f.), that 'Paul's thought-forms can only artificially be restricted to the forensic', that 'righteousness on the divine side is ultimately God's fidelity to his creation', and therefore that 'the many have been *made* righteous in the sense that the primal creation bond has been renewed: the image of God has been restored, resulting in a basic change of attitude on the part of those who have been reconciled to God.' Logically, this leads him to write: 'Beker is correct that the historic debate concerning *gratia imputata* [imputed grace] versus *gratia infusa* [imparted grace] bypasses Paul's basic intent' (p. 76 n. 13; *cf.* p. 74, 'The essential difference between him [Paul] and the Jewish outlook lay just in his conviction that, in Christ, the eschaton had

15ff. would not dispel the objection, for the difference (in the apostle's eyes) relates to the effect, to the scale of the consequences, not to the way the role or cause operates. While we cannot demand perfect formal correspondence, there must be enough for some symmetry to obtain.

The crux, or the nut too hard to crack, is found in verses 13–14, Paul's digression in support of his statement at the end of verse 12. For those whose interpretative strategy concentrates on the fact that all people sin, the apostle's emphasis on the case of those who did *not* sin after the likeness of Adam's transgression is somewhat puzzling. Why does Paul make this detour into the pre-Mosaic period? How is he then led to see Adam as a type of Christ?

Bultmann (1952: 252)[9] seems to throw in the sponge: 'Verse 13 is completely unintelligible.' In Dunn's eyes (1988: 275), Paul could have answered the objection by referring to the law of Romans 1, yet he did not, and this 'must be significant . . . What the significance is, however, remains unclear.' Lyonnet (1963: 556f.) imagines someone afflicted with too narrow a juridical mind raising the objection that in the absence of a law, sin is not imputed – an objection which Paul dismisses in verse 14, his argument being simply that the facts of God's judgment prove the opposite. But the principle of verse 13b, a fundamental point of law, is Paul's own; he laid it down in 4:15. Paul's own mind is intensely juridical.

Those solutions look strained that either affirm the presence of a law such as would guarantee that sin entails death,[10] or deny that sin was reckoned. The former clash with Paul's unequivocal words, 'there was no law', and, to a degree, diverge from his stress on sin unlike Adam's. The difference may not be reduced

---

arrived'). I rather feel that such an outlook bypasses the burning core of Paul's gospel, his passionate paradox of the justification of the ungodly, his rigorous analysis of its conditions (Rom. 3 – 4; Gal. 3) and his most decisive presuppositions.

[9] I was led to this reference by Dunn 1988: 274.

[10] Leon Morris (1988: 234) ascribes such a choice to R. A. Harrisville. Garlington (1994: 96) proposes: 'A law has been spurned, a law which functions similarly to the *nomos* which works wrath. However, it is not the law of the Sinai covenant, as in 4:15; it is, rather, some law in existence before the birth of Israel's nationhood . . .'

to a question of mode, or to triviality.[11] The latter solution
ascribes to the apostle a most improbable thought: 'On biblical
premises, it can scarcely be denied that sin was reckoned to
people and punished in the period between Adam and Moses,
as the flood narrative, to name no other, plainly shows (Gen 6:5–
7, 12–13)' (Morris 1988: 233).[12]

Cranfield (1975: 282) bravely faces the situation and evaluates
the data. He is worth quoting at length:

> By *ouk ellogeitai* ['is not reckoned'] Paul does not mean
> that [sin] is not registered in the sense of being
> charged to men's account, reckoned against them,
> imputed; for the fact that men died during this period
> of the law's absence (v. 14) shows clearly enough that
> in this sense their sin was indeed registered. *Ouk
> ellogeitai* must be understood in a relative sense: only in
> comparison with what takes place when the law is
> present can it be said that, in the law's absence, sin *ouk
> ellogeitai*. Those who lived without the law were
> certainly not 'innocent sinners' – they were to blame
> for what they were and what they did. But, in
> comparison with the state of affairs which has obtained
> since the advent of the law, sin may be said to have
> been, in the law's absence, 'not registered', since it was
> not the fully apparent, sharply defined thing, which it
> became in its presence.

Such relativizing, however, carries its own risk. A juridical
category such as imputation hardly admits of degrees; either sin
is reckoned or it is not. The strong adversative at the beginning
of verse 14, *alla*, 'on the contrary, nevertheless', is not easily
explained on Cranfield's terms. In his perspective, this *alla*, as
he writes himself, is 'at first sight rather surprising' (p. 282).
Douglas Moo (1991: 341) underlines the fact that reducing
verse 13b to the 'status of a rather negligible aside' cannot be

---

[11] As Garlington does (1994: 97): 'They did not do *precisely* what Adam did,
i.e., eat a piece of forbidden fruit in the Garden of Eden.'

[12] On this point, Garlington (1994: 96) is happily firm: '*ellogeitai* does have to
do with individual responsibility. The other Pauline occurrence of *ellogeō* is
Phlm 18, where the apostle assumes personal accountability for the debt of
Onesimus.'

sustained.[13] When Moo, in spite of the pointed criticisms he has levelled at Cranfield's position, reluctantly joins his party, he himself becomes vulnerable on the theme of imputation (pp. 344f.).[14] Within the framework of Paul's theology, I would maintain, death follows upon sin first and foremost in the logic of retributive justice, as the judicial 'payment' for sin (Rom. 6:23). In Romans 5, at least, this must be the case, since the reign of death is based on condemnation (vv. 16–17, cf. 21),[15] and it is one and the same thing to reckon sin and to condemn the sinner. In chapters 1 – 3, Paul's indictment of the whole human race, placed under condemnation (3:19, *hypodikos*), is based upon the presence of law written on the Gentiles' hearts as well as in Israel's special revelation. All contextual clues appear unfavourable to the solutions of the 'looser' exegetes on the crux verses 13 and 14.

Further weaknesses would surface under closer examination: such as a tendency among the first group of interpreters to separate the sinful bent from real guilt – a tendency uncongenial to biblical sensitivity. But the problem of verses 13–14, together with the other critical considerations summarized here, is enough to impel the search for another reading.

Tighter interpretations of Romans 5

The Augustinian line on Romans 5, to which Moo (1991: 338) assigns 'a great number of exegetes and theologians', boldly sees in Adam a negative image of most of what we know of justification's *modus operandi*. By virtue of Christ's headship, and of our being 'in him', his righteousness, which is alien to us, is reckoned to our account. Similarly, by virtue of Adam's headship, and of our being 'in him', his sin and guilt, which

[13] Moo emphasizes Paul's *alla*.

[14] Moo falls back into distinguishing degrees of sin: 'Sin can be charged explicitly and in detail to each person's account only when that person has consciously and knowingly disobeyed a direct command that prohibits that sin' (p. 345). Do we discover enough scriptural and Pauline evidence to support this claim? Similar weakening of the biblical viewpoint is found in Garlington 1994: 86 n. 60, agreeing with Dunn.

[15] *Contra* Dunn 1988: 276: 'Whatever the precise relation Paul has in mind between death as consequence of human sinfulness and death as "payment" for sin (6:23; see on 5:13), it is certainly the former he has in mind here [5:14].' This distinction seems to me entirely artificial.

are alien to us, are reckoned to our account. The logic of our participation in Christ ('One died for all, therefore all have died', 2 Cor. 5:14)[16] also governs Romans 5:12d: one sinned for all, therefore all have sinned. 'All have sinned' in Eden, in Adam's person. Through Adam sin entered the world. How did death, the judicial payment for sin, follow? Since Adam's sin was not only his own 'private' transgression but that of the whole race – since all have sinned in the one disobedience of Genesis 3 – death spread to all.

The case does not (contrary to a superficial understanding of the issues) rest on the rendering of the connecting words at the end of verse 12 for which Augustine finally settled. He understood *eph' hō* to mean *in quo*, 'in whom', that is, in Adam. It cannot be justified, however, to pour contempt on his choice as a 'fatal blunder'.[17] Some modern authorities (N. Turner, W. Manson) still defend it. Fitzmyer's panoramic treatment (1993: 332ff.) shows that none of the many rival solutions is unassailable, including the majority rendering 'because, inasmuch as'. Fitzmyer's own proposal, 'with the result that', although philologically possible, apparently reverses the order between sin and death.[18] Lyonnet's solution (1963: 544ff.) – 'the condition being fulfilled that' – seems one of the most attractive, or least objectionable; but it is not far in meaning from the common and convenient 'because'.[19] Whatever the choice, it does not preclude an Augustinian interpretation of the whole passage.

How are all humans to be seen 'in Adam'? Augustine championed the so-called 'realistic' view, taking his cue from Hebrews 7:10 (Levi, being in Abraham's loins, paid the tithe to Melchizedek) – all future human individuals were in Adam's loins 'seminally'. The emphasis falls on Adam's position as the progenitor of the race. Another version, which betrays some influence of philosophical idealism, focuses on human 'nature', which was wholly in Adam and fell with him.[20] Reformed theology, without denying the natural connection, highlights

---

[16] A verse appealed to, *e.g.*, by Turretin 1847: 565 (IX.9.28).

[17] As Williams (1927: 379) does when he says that Augustine 'misinterpreted' Rom. 5:12 in accordance with 'Ambrosiaster's fatal blunder'.

[18] He reviews eleven other options, pp. 322–328.

[19] Moo (1991: 333f.), having made a careful survey, accepts 'because'.

[20] William Shedd pioneered the new conception, was followed by Augustus Strong (1907: 619ff.). Strong quotes Shedd approvingly as having written: 'We

the judicial capacity of Adam as covenant head and racial representative who was called to act in the name of humankind. We were 'in him' in the sense of being legally represented by him. Turretin, 'the Protestant Thomas Aquinas', powerfully elaborated this doctrinal structure.[21] It has been maintained by most Calvinistic theologians, and further refined by John Murray (1977).

The meaning of 'all have sinned' in Romans 5:12d is decisive here. May we depart from what most regard as the 'natural' sense?[22] Turretin (1847: 559 [IX.9.16, 3]) argued from the aorist tense (*hēmarton*) that it could not refer to habitual sin or to the state of corruption, but rather pointed to one act of sinning. S. Lewis Johnson and Leon Morris take up the argument,[23] and so, even more emphatically, does P. E. Hughes, who extends its application to Romans 3:23 explained as follows: 'All sinned (aorist) when Adam sinned and fall short (present) of the glory of God in their own personal conduct' (1989: 130). With due respect to these scholars, it is noticeable that grammarians are slow to countenance their claim. The Greek aorist tense or aspect is susceptible of various uses: culminative, complexive, gnomic. Edward de Witt Burton (1894: 28, para. 54) summed up the matter with admirable precision: in Romans 5:12 the aorist *hēmarton* may refer to a past deed at a given moment of time, or it may bear the same nuance as in 3:23, where it 'is evidently intended to sum up the aggregate of the evil deeds of men'. In 5:12, 'so far as the tense-form is concerned there is no presumption in favour of one or the other of these interpreta-

---

all existed in Adam in our elementary invisible substance. The *Seyn* of all was there, though the *Daseyn* was not; the *noumenon*, though not the *phenomenon*, was in existence' (p. 621, no reference). See Murray (1977: 24–36) for an excellent presentation and critique of the 'realistic view'. Hughes (1989: 131f.) takes up the idea of human nature fallen ('the humanness of our nature, whether concentrated in one individual or distributed among many . . .') but his position is less than crystal clear as he warns: 'We are speaking of human nature not as a quantity or a dimension but as an existential reality.' Johnson (1974: 308 with n. 73) cites James H. Thornwell (debated), S. Greijdanus and Klaas Schilder as supporters of the 'realist' view.

[21] See Turretin 1847: 517 (VIII.3), 554f. (IX.9) and *passim*.

[22] Berkouwer (1971: 499) quotes from Greijdanus' objection: Paul did not write *eph' hō pantes hamartanein elogisthēsan*, 'in that all are reckoned to sin'.

[23] Johnson (1974: 306 n. 50) says the reference to the actual sins of all 'would seem to demand the present tense'. See also Morris 1988: 231.

tions, both uses of the tense being equally legitimate'. Stanley Porter (1990a: 25) advises not to look for a punctiliar aorist: 'It is probably an omnitemporal statement.'

The most interesting parallel passage is found in the Septuagint, at Leviticus 4:3. Surprisingly, it is seldom referred to.[24] The same verb 'to sin', *hamartanein*, is used in the aorist tense for the people's state of *'āšām* (guilt) in consequence of the high priest's fault. The idea of 'corporate' sin seems to emerge from this; the New English Bible renders: 'If the anointed priest sins so as to bring guilt on the people . . .' This fits with the Augustinian reading of Romans 5:12. We should proceed cautiously, however, since *hamartanein* rarely corresponds to *'āšām*, and the notion of *'āšām* may not lead us far beyond the notion of a mere penalty undergone or consequences suffered – not real guilt incurred.[25]

The spearhead of the main Reformed interpretation, that of Turretin and his successors, is the rather provocative thesis that inherited corruption *follows* upon the imputation of Adam's sin as an integral part of the penalty. Because of Adam's federal headship, his transgression is charged to the account of his descendants; before they are conceived, they are condemned and sentenced to death (separation from God, v. 12c). They are thus conceived in sin, with a corrupt nature. Turretin boldly claims that this is the only way to vindicate God's justice in condemning them.[26] Immediate imputation, in Johnson's eloquent summary (1974: 12), 'is implied in man's estate, born spiritually dead and evidently under a curse (*cf.* Eph. 2:1–5). He was either tried in Adam and fell, or he has been condemned without a trial. He is under a curse for Adam's guilt, or for no guilt at all.'

The argument is not devoid of force. Yet it requires 'death' to be understood primarily in spiritual terms – death as inflicted before birth, before conception. Is this thought likely here in Paul? Charles Hodge himself, chief among the followers of

---

[24] Only Ligier (1961: 273ff.) deals with it at some length.

[25] In Joel 1:18 (MT), after the plague of locusts and through want of rain, the flocks *nĕšāmû* (NIV, 'are suffering').

[26] 'Negata imputatione immediata primi peccati, praecipuum fundamentum justitiae propagationis peccati tollitur' ('If one denies the immediate imputation of the first sin, one removes the main ground for showing that the propagation of sin is just') (1847: 562 [IX.9.21]).

Turretin, had to acknowledge that 'natural death . . . no doubt was prominent in the apostle's mind, as appears from vs. 13, 14' (1838: 133).[27] Paul uses the obvious phenomenon of the universal reign of death 'from Adam to Moses' in verse 14 to prove his point: death in the daily 'physical' sense – at the end, not at the beginning, of earthly existence. The parallel chapter, 1 Corinthians 15, provides weighty confirmation: 'In Adam all die' must refer there to death of the body, since the whole discussion is devoted to the disputed issue of bodily resurrection.

The Augustinian, especially Reformed, interpretation of Romans 5 achieves a remarkable degree of consistency and prevails, in my estimation, over its traditional rivals. But it is not immune to criticism. In this line of argument also, curiously, the central link is not explicit in the text. Although verse 12d *may* be construed as an allusion to the imputation to all people of Adam's misdeed – is it the most natural reading? – nowhere else is that thought distinctly expressed.

This situation is all the more disconcerting in that it is precisely this point that arouses the fiercest protests.[28] Though Turretin (1847: 561 [IX.9.19]) pleads that the imputation of alien sins is frequent and regular in Scripture, and even adduces the witness of heathen culture, it cannot be denied that the concept sits uneasily with our sense of personal responsibility – not only modern, but in a biblically formed sense.[29] Johnson (1974: 315) candidly admits: 'We do not for one moment belittle the problem of the *peccatum alienum*, acknowledging that it tends

---

[27] Most commentators perceive a reference to bodily death, though not exclusively: 'Physical death is in mind, but not physical death in itself; it is physical death as the sign and symbol of spiritual death' (Morris 1988: 228). Dunn (1988: 273) denies a distinction here; Moo (1991: 332) sees both aspects. For the opposite view see Malina 1969: 29 n. 34, and n. 35 for opponents. Cranfield (1975: II, 844f.) offers a fine excursus on 'Death Understood as the Consequence of Sin', in which he argues that it is 'not necessarily obscurantist to believe' that man disobediently rejected a possibility of life exempt from the necessity of death (in the ordinary sense of 'death').

[28] Moo (1991: 339 n. 41) recalls, for example, Pannenberg's vehement reaction.

[29] Turretin (1847: 564ff. [IX.9.26f.]) labours hard to reconcile his teaching with Dt. 24:16 and Ezk. 18:20; on the latter passage, he argues: 'Ita non hic fit ulla *juris definitio*, sed tantum *pactis specialis declaratio*'; 'Thus here he does not make any legal judgment, but rather declares a special covenant.'

to weaken the case for immediate imputation.' The perfect symmetry between grace and justice, between the undeserved gift of righteousness and responsibility for alien sin, is not as self-evident as is often claimed (Turretin 1847: 563 [IX.9.23]). As to the idea of human nature as an 'invisible substance', a thing in itself, which can be 'concentrated' or 'distributed', this smacks more of philosophy than of biblical theology; to give it an important structural role, more scriptural warrant would be needed.[30]

A more detailed analysis of communal liability might be relevant.[31] Perhaps we should distinguish between two possible kinds of such liability. On the one hand, there is the idea of suffering the consequences of another's sin, especially that of the community's head; it is his punishment, and since the community belongs to him, he is stricken through what he owns. On the other hand, there is the idea of reckoning alien guilt to the community members, involving their condemnation. Johnson ignores the distinction,[32] but, in this regard, Kirwan (1988: 137) exposes the 'confusion between compensation and punishment, or between debt and guilt'. The concept of liability as debt incurring payment of compensation does appear frequently in Scripture, and throughout human history. But David's admirable plea and confession in 2 Samuel 24:17 does not suggest imputation of alien guilt: 'It is I who have done wrong, the sin is mine; but these poor sheep, what have they done?'

And so back to the crux of verses 13–14. The Reformed interpretation of Romans 5 is able to explain clearly in what respects Adam typifies Christ, and why death reigned independently, or rather *antecedently*, of the actual sins of people. Yet there remains a slight tension between Paul's wording, 'they did not sin after the likeness of Adam's transgression', and the Reformed emphasis that they sinned in Adam. Moreover, Reformed commentators are puzzled by the special place the

---

[30] Jacques Liébaert (1975: 51) underlines that the fathers usually mean 'humankind' when they say 'human nature' (*physis*), with the relative exception of Gregory of Nyssa.

[31] See the interesting remarks, from the legal point of view, in Théry 1975: 130–152.

[32] Johnson (1974: 312 n. 100) observes, 'It is just as "unjust" to bear the consequences of the guilt of someone else as it is to bear the guilt itself.' Is it?

apostle gives to the period from Adam to Moses in his argument. Obviously, it does not make much sense for them. John Murray offers the following paraphrase of verse 13:

> Although it is true that from Adam to Moses sin was in the world *and therefore law*, though thus there was sin such as would explain the presence of death, yet in that period death reigned not only over those who were violators of expressly revealed law, as was Adam, but also over those who did not sin in that manner, that is, after the pattern of Adam (1967: 189f., my italics).

He makes a noticeable departure from the text. Affirming the existence of a law apparently conflicts with Paul's statement, and a distinction of categories among those who lived between Adam and Moses has to be read into verse 14. Instead of recognizing all sinners in the period as those who did not sin like Adam, Murray still clings to the view that marks out the latter as a distinct group, whom he identifies as infants and mentally handicapped persons (pp. 190f.). Romans 5 does not contain the slightest hint of such a reference, which nearly all recent interpreters discard unhesitatingly.[33] Murray himself confesses: 'We may not be able to determine the precise scope of the classification' (p. 191 n. 23). Could this be the symptom of a misreading somewhere?

Untying the knot? A new interpretation

When the two rival approaches that together hold the field still fail to satisfy, it is worth asking whether they could share a hidden, *uncriticized* presupposition – valid or not. It is easy to take as self-evident things which are not so; maybe the apostle's subtlety and foreign ways of thinking have been underestimated. Malina (1969: 27) stresses that his style in Romans 5 is 'typically

---

[33] See Cranfield 1975: I, 279; Dunn 1988: 276; Moo 1991: 343. It seems to be the most conspicuous weakness in Johnson's article (1974: 310) that he has still to introduce a class 'composed of infants and idiots' (although he adds, 'it seems').

scribal or "early rabbinic" '; one striking feature is the place of legal terminology.[34]

Both kinds of interpretations, looser and tighter, appear to share a disjunctive presupposition: *either* we are condemned for our own sins (and Adam's role is reduced to that of a remote fountainhead, losing much of its significance) *or* we are condemned for his sin (and the equity of that transfer is hard to see). Now, what if this 'either/or' were misleading? What if there were a third possibility?

Today we tend to take condemnation for our own sins as a matter of simple logic. But verse 13b (*cf.* 4:15) shows that this was not the case for Paul's acute theologico-juridical mind. Without a law, sin is undefined, *apeiron*; it cannot be made the object of judgment. My hypothesis, then, is as follows: I submit that the role of Adam and of his sin in Romans 5 is *to make possible the imputation, the judicial treatment, of human sins.* His role thus brings about the condemnation of all, and its sequel, death.

If persons are considered individually, they have no standing with God, no relationship to his judgment. They are, as it were, floating in a vacuum. Sin cannot be imputed. But God sees them in Adam and through Adam, in the framework of the covenant of creation. Therefore he sees their sins as committed against the Genesis 2 command, as grafted on to Adam's sin in Eden. Before the law of Moses was promulgated, sin was imputed and therefore death reigned owing to the relationship of all humans to Adam, the natural and legal head or mediator.[35] How did the

---

[34] My appreciation of that feature leads me in the opposite direction to Garlington's effort at a new interpretation. He tends to erase the legal thought-forms. For him, 'Adam and Christ correspond typologically as creators of their respective races, with each community bearing the image of its creator' (1994: 100); 'If like begets like, the *dikaioi* are those in whom *Christ* has been reproduced' (p. 107); 'Christ thus plays out the role originally assigned to Adam as the progenitor of the human race' (p. 108); on Adam's side at least, the emphasis falls on imitation (pp. 85, 87f., 103f.). I fail to perceive these emphases in Rom. 5.

[35] Actually, Turretin (1847: 560 [IX.9.17]), in spite of his reference to infants, comes quite near to this hypothesis: 'Quia vero imputatio peccati ad poenam non potest fieri non existente Lege . . . Paulus inde elicit, legem ergo aliquam datam fuisse ante Legem scriptam Mosis, juxta quam peccatum potest dici imputatum; *quae non potest alia esse, quam Lex primordialis lata Adamo et in eo omnibus posteris ejus*' ('Since, truly, one cannot make a penal imputation of sin while there exists no law. . . . Paul brings to light that, prior to the written Law of

punishment, death, reach all persons on the basis of (*eph' hō*) their actual sinning? It reached them in the same way that death entered Adam's person: since all were in Adam, the head, sin could be reckoned to them according to the terms of the Adamic covenant, as offshoots of his sin. This is manifest in the period before Moses when there was no law which rendered imputation possible independently of Adam (vv. 13f.).

The hypothesis accounts for the choice of the period, and it does seem to make for a smooth reading. A paraphrase of the passage becomes easy:

> Just as through one man, Adam, sin entered the world and the sin–death connection was established, and so death could be inflicted on all as the penalty of their sins . . .
>
> For take the period from Adam to Moses: sin was in the world, yet sin is not imputed in the absence of law, when it is viewed independently; nevertheless it was imputed through the relationship of all to Adam, and so death reigned even over people who had not sinned, as Adam had done, by violating a precept directly given to them. Adam's role as a racial head for condemnation makes him a type of Christ, the Head for justification.
>
> Of course, the operation of grace in Christ is infinitely more powerful. It miraculously reverses a desperate situation marred by millions of sins,[36] whereas Adam's role is to secure condemnation of condemnable deeds.
>
> Yet it can be said that through the one disobedience of Adam, of which all human sins are offshoots, all

---

Moses, some law must have been given, according to which one can say that sin was reckoned, and *which can be no other than the primordial Law enacted for Adam and for all his descendants'*) (my italics). He does not seem to see, however, that *Adam*'s role in Paul's argument is to provide that substitute of Moses' law. We should avoid speaking of 'law', a potentially misleading word in the exegesis of Rom. 5:13f., and stress covenant solidarity.

[36] Cranfield (1975: I, 286) writes magnificently: 'That one single misdeed should be answered by judgment, that is perfectly understandable: that the accumulated sins and guilt of all the ages should be answered by God's free gift, this is the miracle of miracles, utterly beyond human comprehension.'

have been constituted sinners, just as through the one obedience of Christ all who own him as their Head are constituted righteous.

The wording of verse 16 agrees well with the idea: the effect of the one offence is to ensure that the judgment verdict, *krima*, is condemnation, *katakrima*.[37] Paul's additional comment on the role of the law (of Moses) in verse 20 is perfectly in line with the reading: the law played a part similar in kind to that of Adam's headship; it was not indispensable for imputation (because of Adam), but it increased the efficacy of the reckoning of sin.

This hypothesis also highlights Paul's *aim* throughout the whole comparison. It was not, as Murray suggests (1967: 179) – and Turretin before him (1847: 558 [IX.9.16]) – to explain God's method of justification. Nor was it, as Cranfield stresses,[38] to bring out the universality of Christ's redemptive benefits. Moo (1991: 302) has more accurately captured Paul's concern in Romans 5:

> But can that verdict [justification], hidden to the senses, guarantee that one will be delivered from God's wrath when it is poured out in judgment? Yes, affirms Paul. Nothing can stand in its way: not death (5:12–21), not sin (chap. 6), not the law (chap. 7) – nothing! (chap. 8). What God has begun, having justified and reconciled us, He will bring to a triumphant conclusion and save us from wrath.

Ligier (1961: 257) had already recognized the scope of the passage: 'The doctrine of the two Adams is put forward to show that Christ's death not only achieved reconciliation through the gift of righteousness now, but also opened, in view of the future and for all, salvation and the kingdom.'

[37] See Cranfield 1975: I, 287 n. 1 on the two words and their nuances.
[38] 'The purpose of the comparison is to make clear the universal range of what Christ has done' (1975: I, 281, *cf.* 269, 271 n. 5). Dunn (1988: 273) is more restrained. Garlington (1994: 80) wanders in another direction: 'The Adam/Christ analogy is intended to ground the perseverance of the saints in the perseverance (obedience) of Christ himself . . .' He realizes, however, that deliverance from wrath was not a self-evident consequence of justification (p. 78).

A 'refrain' witnesses to the unity of the whole chapter (while it also enhances the rabbinic flavour of Paul's reasoning, since it corresponds to the *qal w^{a}hômēr* hermeneutical rule): 'how much more', *pollō mallon.* The text offers us that key four times (vv. 9, 10, 15, 17), and the idea emerges once more with the 'overabundance' of verse 20 (*hypereperisseusen*). Since justification has been established in chapters 3 and 4 (hence 5:1, 'Being, therefore, justified . . .'), the issue is now that of assurance, of the fullness of the life to come as a sure inheritance. And the grand parallel with Adam serves as the grounding of that assurance: if Adam's role was so dramatically efficacious in securing the condemnation of all people in him, and therefore the reign of death, how much more is Christ's work efficacious for those in him, leading to life eternal!

The hypothesis I propose easily accounts for the imperfect symmetry between the two heads of humankind. Adam's role is more firmly cast than in the 'looser' reading of Romans 5; at the same time, the unattested and difficult thesis of the imputation of an *alien* sin is avoided – without downplaying the tragic realism of the Augustinian human predicament.

One major objection could arise. If this objection is valid, I readily acknowledge that the whole construction falls to pieces. It runs thus: Adam's role is not the only possible ground of the divine imputation of sins before Moses; there is also the law of Romans 2, and it does function in that way in Romans 2 – 3. The heathen who are without the law of Moses stand condemned on the basis of the law written upon their hearts.

The answer is brief. Certainly the law of Romans 2 functions in this way – but is that word 'also' correct? Is that law an additional ground? I agree with the interpretation of chapters 2 and 3 which the objection implies. The heathen are a law for themselves (2:14); if this provides a way other than that of Adamic dependence, leading to the same end (imputation of human sins), then my proposal must be withdrawn. But I venture to suggest that it is not 'another' way; rather, it is the same way described from another angle. Being related to God through Adam, the covenant head, is equivalent to having the law written on one's heart; they are two sides of the same coin. 'Since the publication of M. D. Hooker's [1959–60] article "Adam in Romans 1", scholars have been aware that Paul's depiction of man and his plight is modeled on the fall of Adam in Genesis' (Garlington 1994: 34). Such an insight should be applied to the second chapter as well. The law of Romans 2, a sense of God's demands built into our very constitution, is ours *as the children of Adam*. This anthropological privilege derives from our creation through Adam and in Adam. Therefore the apostle is referring to the same reality, first in the categories of experience analysed (Rom. 2), and secondly in the categories of *Heilsgeschichte*, redemptive history (Rom. 5) – first 'synchronically', and secondly according to 'diachronic' sequence. In other words, responsibility is radically Adamic, with a reflection, a trace, a witness, in the heart we inherit from Adam.

Paradoxically, this hypothesis entails that Paul was not dealing directly with original sin, at least *originated* original sin, in Romans 5. This does not mean that the reality of transmitted corruption and guilt attached to every human life from the womb was not in the background of his argument, or that Romans 5 in the new reading has no bearing on the doctrine of original sin. The possible consequences of the new thesis will be explored in the concluding (more dogmatic) chapter, but first we turn to the witness of human experience.

Chapter Four

Original sin as a key to human experience

Blaise Pascal, the greatest Christian genius (with John Calvin) that it was granted to France to bring forth, jotted down the following notes on the riddle of human character:

> (Of man) If he boasts, I humiliate him,
> If he is humble, I vaunt him;
> And contradict him always,
> Until he comes to understand
> That he is an incomprehensible monster (1962: 167).[1]

What sort of a monster then is man? What a novelty, what a portent, what a chaos, what a mass of contradictions, what a prodigy! Judge of all things, a ridiculous earthworm who is the repository of truth, a sink of uncertainty and error; the glory and the scum of the world.

Who shall unravel such a tangle? . . .

Nature confounds the sceptics, and reason confounds the dogmatists . . .

Know then, proud man, what a paradox you are to yourself. Humble yourself, impotent reason; be silent, dull-witted nature, and learn from your master your true condition which you do not know. Listen to God . . .

It is an astonishing thing, however, that the mystery which is furthest removed from our knowledge – the mystery of the transmission of sin – is something without which we can have no knowledge of ourselves!

For there is no doubt that there is nothing that shocks our reason more than to say that the sin of the

---

[1] *Pensée* 245 in Lafuma's classification and 420 in Brunschvicg's.

first man was the cause of the guilt of those who were so far from the source of infection that it seems impossible that they should have been contaminated by it. The transmission of sin seems to us not only impossible, it even seems very unjust; for what could be more contrary to the rules of our sorry justice than the eternal damnation of a child incapable of will-power for a sin in which he seems to have played so small a part, and which was committed six thousand years before he was born? Nothing, to be sure, is more of a shock to us than such a doctrine and yet, without this mystery, which is the most incomprehensible of all, we should be incomprehensible to ourselves. The tangled knot of our condition acquired its twists and turns in that abyss; so that man is more inconceivable without the mystery than the mystery is to man (pp. 169f.).[2]

'Illuminating the riddle': the first meaning intended by this volume's sub-title is simply an echo of Pascal's overwhelming argument. Following his line, after we have studied scriptural foundations of the doctrine, we should perceive how that doctrine sheds light on and into human darkness, and how it accounts for the tangles and knots of experience.

Such an attempt causes our exploration in dogmatics to verge on apologetics. After all, the *Pensées* are notes and drafts which Pascal planned to work up into an apology for Christianity. 'Niebuhr was fond of quoting the assertion of the . . . *Times Literary Supplement*, "The doctrine of original sin is the only empirically verifiable doctrine of the Christian faith."'[3] The statement should not be taken literally – universal experience confirms many other doctrines – but it is suggestive. My hope is that this enquiry will enhance the persuasive power of the doctrine, which I consider to be basically biblical. The main objective, however, remains to understand the meaning and reference of scriptural teaching more precisely.

How can we proceed? Ideally, by surveying the whole field of

---

[2] *Pensée* 246 (Lafuma), 434 (Brunschvicg).

[3] Quoted by Peters 1994: 326, from (Reinhold) Niebuhr's *Man's Nature and His Communities* (New York: Scribner's, 1965), p. 24.

human experience, and comparing and testing against it the various models that have been devised to account for the phenomena. The 'original sin' model could then be shown to fit the facts, or at least, to fit them better than any rival theory. But even if this were possible, I do not consider 'empirical fit' to be the last word in method. Such a complex, mobile, all-encompassing, immense object as 'experience' can be apprehended only within a 'fideistic' framework, a structure of presuppositions, in the arrangement of prior patterns and horizons, and under the control of 'ground-motives'.[4]

We must, therefore, be selective. This chapter will focus on the paradoxical *dualities* in experience which are closely related to the main articles of our doctrine. The dualities interact and overlap, so that some of the following sub-divisions may appear artificial. Yet they may count as helpful samples of the enigmas of human life which – I believe, following Pascal – the doctrine of original sin is alone able to illuminate. The endeavour enjoys biblical precedent, for wisdom literature also appeals to experience in support of revealed doctrine (the fear of the LORD) and in applying it. The book of Ecclesiastes has a special interest in riddles and paradoxes (see Goldsworthy 1987). Paul's address to the Areopagus (Acts 17:22ff.) provides a New Testament model of wisdom in the service of truth.

Misery and royal descent

Since Pascal has opened the way, let us follow in his steps. The riddle which divine revelation alone is able to unlock is that of the *misery* and the *nobility* of humankind. Humans demonstrate baseness of all kinds (first and foremost moral and spiritual) and yet traits that witness to royal descent.

Something is rotten not only in the state of Denmark but in human life universally. Who can deny the presence of evil, insidious or oppressive, on all hands? Words are inadequate to describe the hold of evil over our world, the web of lust and lies,

---

[4] The reader will easily spot here a 'neo-Calvinistic' orientation, with allusions to Cornelius Van Til (presuppositions) and Herman Dooyeweerd (ground-motives); more recently Lesslie Newbigin has taken a similar approach, drawing on Michael Polanyi (fideistic framework) whose epistemological contribution also influenced Thomas F. Torrance. Developing the point would lead us beyond the scope of this study.

the endless inventions of forms of torture, the host of sufferings and cruelties that fill the earth as the waters fill the sea. Countless preachers have attempted to do justice to it. Ted Peters' (1994) treatment, with case stories and testimonies, goes very far along the way. Perhaps it is enough to open our daily newspapers, or to turn to our greatest artists. Certainly, the world resembles Albert Camus's city of Oran, infected with *The Plague*, and sensitive people who begin to ponder their own responsibilities in this do not escape *The Fall* (by the same writer) into the abyss of self-accusation, the hell of a guilty conscience.

The century of Auschwitz and the Gulag, as it comes to a close, cannot close its eyes to this state of affairs. It has been fully demonstrated, especially, that the worst of torturers do not belong to a separate category of 'monsters'. Most of them had been 'decent' people, ordinary folk, good neighbours, good fathers. Circumstances brought to light what they were capable of doing. This was true of Treblinka's SS. It was true of policemen in the Gulag system of communist Bulgaria: 'In other circumstances,' Todorov (1992: 37) discerns, 'they would not have behaved as sadists; they are just ordinary people who have found there an easy way to taste the pleasures of power.'[5]

Seemingly unaware of the possible connection, Todorov's comments on the former regime in eastern Europe bring strong support for the doctrine of original sin. He writes: 'Totalitarianism is now dead in Europe not because it was not "good" (an unjust society may endure indefinitely) but because it was not "true", or, more accurately, because it rested on hypotheses regarding man's nature and society which proved to be false' (p. 27). The evidence we have been recalling surely belies what has been for centuries the rival doctrine in the western world: *optimism.*

The liberal 'bourgeois' version of progress optimism collapsed in catastrophe when the so-called civilized countries slaughtered millions of young men in the First World War blood-bath, a mass sacrifice to the idol of national pride. At the same time, psychoanalysis had started to discover in the hidden depths of personality, in the unconscious of the most respectable citizens,

---

[5] The book is a moving collection of testimonies from victims, with an admirable introduction by Todorov (pp. 9–53).

'a veritable hell' (in Freud's own words),[6] a horrendous mixture of murderous drives and incestuous desires. For his *Traumdeutung* (*The Interpretation of Dreams*) in 1900, the inaugural work or firstfruits of psychoanalysis, Freud had chosen as his epigraph Virgil's line from the *Aeneid*: *Flectere si nequeo Superos, Acheronta movebo*,[7] 'If I cannot sway the Higher Powers, I will stir up the Underworld', an allusion both to the repressed feelings or wishes within the unconscious and to Freud's own action despite the cool welcome he would receive on the part of official science (Mannoni, 1968: 84). A little later, the worldwide economic crisis ruined whatever illusions remained. In that context, the heir of the liberal 'social gospel', Reinhold Niebuhr, went back to the doctrine of original sin, which he reinterpreted under the label 'realistic theology'.

Other versions of optimism fare little better. The revolutionary type crumbled in a few years, with the Berlin wall as its symbol. The failure of all Marxist regimes to fulfil their promises has left a yawning ideological vacuum; it is hard to imagine today the burning conviction and sacrificial zeal of communist militants only thirty years ago. This competitor is in retreat. But is the technocratic optimism of our western elites more solidly grounded? The condition of our cities the world over, the morals of youth in most countries, and the statistics of unemployment, crime and drug addiction undermine the confidence that social engineering, through policies of unprecedented cost, may decisively curb the factors of evil. Technocratic optimism is based on too superficial a diagnosis of the human predicament.

Optimistic interpretations never die out completely. Like weeds, new forms of illusion spring up continually, through a will to believe born of a will to live. Of reviewing and criticizing them there can be no end.[8] Suffice it to say that the breakdown of the major rivals of the Christian worldview in the twentieth century has created a presumption in favour of the latter.

Yet the optimists do have a case. They can point to real

---

[6] 'These censored wishes seem to rise up from a veritable hell' (Freud 1960: 150).

[7] The title page of the original edition (Leipzig und Wien: Franz Deuticke) is reproduced, for instance, in Mannoni 1968: 82.

[8] Ramm 1985 deals helpfully with several of them *passim* and especially pp. 121ff.

progress in some areas, and not only in material improvement, medicine, education, social programmes and psychotherapy of various sorts. There are beautiful and heroic personalities (among believers and unbelievers) whom we may, indeed should, admire. Even in the midst of wretchedness and wickedness, we can detect a moral reaction still, a nostalgia, a longing, an indignation, a self-loathing, which testify that evil is not the only word – perhaps not the final or the primal word. Even hardened self-satisfaction and moral insensitivity may hide a deeper uneasiness: 'The brutality with which a Pharisee of every age resists those who puncture his pretensions proves the uneasiness of his conscience' (Niebuhr 1941: 256). Pascal's argument carries weight: to know one's base condition is to rise above it.

A striking expression of nostalgia comes from the Romanian-born author Emmanuel Cioran, whose novels and essays paint a dark, destructive picture. (If he did not commit suicide, he once said, it was because death is just as loathsome as life.)

> It would be a torture merely to breathe were it not for the remembrance or the presentiment of Paradise, the supreme object – although unconsciously – of our desires, the unexpressed essence of our memory and of our expectation (1987: 13, as quoted by Gesché 1993: 153).

The evidence of such statements refutes *cynicism*, which is no less a temptation than illusory optimism. Etymologically, 'cynicism' means viewing human beings as *dogs*, and there is a significant trend in our context that tends to do so, to see human beings as 'beyond freedom and dignity'.[9] The cynical inversion glorifies the Pavlovian 'How like a dog!' in place of the Shakespearian and biblical 'How like a god!' Cynicism fails to see that, even when people behave as dogs, or worse than dogs, they are still *not* dogs.

This aspect also belongs to the doctrine of original sin, the first tenet of which is the priority of Genesis 2 over Genesis 3. We must maintain this priority strenuously. Original sin affects the

---

[9] To borrow the phrase, and title, of the famous Harvard behaviourist B. F. Skinner (1980).

good creature of God, and the creature is not annihilated. C. S. Lewis's unguarded language can only be excused as poetic licence when he ventures to write: 'What man lost by the Fall was his original specific nature', and (even worse), 'it was the emergence of a new kind of man – a new species, never made by God, had sinned itself into existence' (1940: 70, 71).[10]

Even the dignity of the divine image remained with humankind, as later scriptures imply (see Blocher 1984: 93f.). Common grace, as Cornelius Van Til (1972) so brilliantly brought to light, embodies God's faithfulness to this primary relationship.[11] Calvin insisted on the efficacy of common grace, a significant counterpoise to pessimistic oversimplifications.[12]

Evangelical preachers ought to pay attention to this element in the teaching of Scripture, and in experience generally. Our temptation may be to exaggerate the situation out of apocalyptic zeal; the more we condemn the world, the more prophetic we feel, or are considered. Kierkegaard (1980: 26) sensed in some traditional articles on original sin, couched in extremely harsh words, 'an almost feminine passion', 'the fanaticism of a girl in love'. Kierkegaard's irony cannot easily be faulted; compared with our own 'evangelical' habits, the balance and sobriety of Scripture are admirable.

Experience, exhibiting the complexity of evil still mixed with some good, of evil resented and reacted against, accords with the doctrine of original sin. But we can go a step further. We can *locate* the operation of evil; or rather refute one-sided, deceptive, locations.

Perhaps the most common strategy of the human mind has been to ascribe the causation of evil to 'lower' elements in our nature. The orientation of Platonism, which weighed so heavily on Christian thought and spirituality, tends to incriminate bodily existence. The apocryphal book of Wisdom, which Augustine read as Scripture, implies this Platonic understanding: 'A

---

[10] This slip of Lewis's strengthens Peter T. Geach's (1977: 133) suspicion of 'a slight Manichean strain in his thought'.

[11] See especially p. 82, 'All common grace is earlier grace', and the fine survey of relevant Scripture passages, pp. 29ff.

[12] Ramm (1985: 119f.) offers a good summary of Calvin's emphases. On the topic, see Kuiper 1928 with an appendix (i–xv) on the views of prominent Reformed theologians, including Abraham Kuyper in the two volumes of his *De Gemeene Gratie*.

perishable body weighs down the soul, and its frame of clay burdens the mind so full of thoughts' (9:15, NEB). Today's strategies focus, rather, on the residue of alleged pre-human stages of evolution, atavistic behaviour no longer adapted to our living conditions. A refined variety of this thinking would be P. D. McLean's theory of our three brains (which Arthur Koestler adopted); our cerebral cortex does not control efficiently our reptilic brain, hence the havoc in persons and society.[13] Vaguer and even more widespread is the feeling that inadequate educational facilities, poverty and bad housing account for misbehaviour. Alternatively, along psychoanalytical lines, one may locate in the *id*, and especially in the death-drive which produces the superego's excessive cruelty, that which causes human beings to suffer unreasonably.

We need not deny the role of such factors. After all, biblical sin can also be analysed in terms of weakness; it means yielding under various pressures, 'leaving it to the snake'.[14] It does involve an ambiguous reversal of created hierarchies, such as that between body and soul. More generally, it involves a disorganization of humankind's exquisite complexity, with functions, instincts and powers given over to uncontrollable divergence. Yet the evidence, carefully investigated, shows that evil attaches supremely to the 'higher' or more central parts of our nature – to the locus of our most precious identity. It supports the biblical insight that what defiles a person comes from the heart. It confirms the doctrine of original sin as a bent in and of the human will, a bondage within freedom. Both Emil Brunner and Reinhold Niebuhr forcefully reminded their generation that human beings sin first and foremost as *spirit*. Brunner (1947: 253) stressed that, for the Christian faith, 'even evil, sin, unbelief, have their seat and their origin in the spirit of man, hence . . . the more spirit there is the greater will be the sin'. Niebuhr (1941: 122) highlighted the dreadful ambivalence of the distinctive privilege of being human:

---

[13] I met the theory first in A. T. W. Simeon's book, *La Psychosomatique, médecine de demain. La lutte contre les 'maladies de civilisation'*, trans. Th. Henrot (Marabout Université. Verviers: Gérard et Cie, 1969), from the English original *Man's Presumptuous Brain* (London: Longmans, Green and Co., 1960).

[14] A phrase inspired by Harvey Cox's title (Cox 1964). Sin, he insists, is first and foremost *acedia*, sloth.

[Idealists fail] to understand the human spirit in its full dimension of freedom. Both the majesty and the tragedy of human life exceed the dimension within which modern culture seeks to comprehend human existence. The human spirit cannot be held within the bounds of either natural necessity or rational prudence. In its yearning towards the infinite lies the source of both human creativity and human sin.[15]

Bernard Ramm (1985: 81f.) eloquently protests (against views currently held) that the evil done by human beings cannot be blamed on vestiges of animality: it goes far beyond anything found among beasts of prey. The Tyger burning bright, in the forests of the night, may stand as a symbol of ferocity, but the symbol pales by comparison with the gruesome reality of humanity. Ramm also gathers pieces of evidence which refute what many people believe: that some professions, especially those which require higher education, 'have a humanizing and moralizing effect upon the members'; physicians, lawyers, politicians, artists, scientists, all use their gifts and skills 'for destructive and immoral purposes' (p. 125). Lord Acton's dictum, 'Power tends to corrupt and absolute power corrupts absolutely', applies beyond the field of politics. Even more accurately, we should say that corruption (of the will) is *already* present; lack of power simply prevents its being manifest, but power allows it expression. Human freedom is turned towards evil; human beings sin if they can, and as much as they can.

Further proof of original sin indwelling the highest abilities of our constitution can be found in the *religious* sphere. Some of the most degrading and inhuman practices have been demanded by worship and inspired by devotion, and this even in the church. The history of Christianity includes frightening chapters. Our twisted hearts deceive with great subtlety: 'There is no final guarantee against the spiritual pride of man. Even the recognition in the sight of God that he is a sinner can be used as a vehicle of that very sin' (Niebuhr 1941: 202). How horribly

[15] *Cf.* his analysis on pp. 188ff. His treatment of Kant is also finely balanced (pp. 118ff.): although 'radical evil' is located in the rational will, under the influence of Christianity (120 n. 12) – and I salute Kant's lucid courage here – still, Niebuhr notes, the sensible self is devalued in an idealistic fashion.

true! And even one's recognition of that truth may be used in the same way. To meet these woeful criticisms, which come also from our own hearts, we have to resort to the old maxim, *Corruptio optimi pessima*, 'the corruption of the best is the worst'.[16] In Shakespeare's words, 'Lilies that fester smell far worse than weeds.' It could well be the secret meaning of 'Antichrist', I would suggest; anti-Christianity is post-Christian sinfulness, which uses the riches of Christ to fuel and intensify human rebellion against God.

Original sin, then, certainly accords with our universal experience.

But there is more to be said about the ugly phenomenon of evil. Analysis, I would recall and claim, shows that evil is perceived and denounced as evil only by reference to the good. There is no isolated experience of evil; rather, under the heading of evil, we note the absence, the deprivation, of a good that ought to be – blindness as the deprivation of sight. When we stand indignantly against unjust treatment, we are actually appealing to standards of equity. Physically as well as morally, we express a sense of wrong when elements of reality are not found in the order we think right, or are not functioning in the way we think sound, or are not used but abused. Such wrongs are against the norm. In knowledge, falsity cannot be conceived apart from its negative reference to the true: *Veritas index sui et falsi*, 'Truth only shows what is true and what is false' (Spinoza). Evil in human experience is secondary, 'parasitic', relative to prior goodness.

The very vocabulary of evil mirrors this character. Most of its words are constructed with negative or privative prefixes: *in*justice, *dis*order, *mis*fortune, *mis*chief . . . In the history of Christian thought, Augustine seized upon this insight to free himself from Manichean influence, and developed the doctrine of evil as deprivation, corruption, perversion, of the good.

This is part of the doctrine of original sin. For it interprets evil in human experience as *fallenness*. It dispels as a subtle and pernicious lie the symmetrical opposition of good and evil in dualistic systems. Such an opposition looks most radical; it would seem to declare uncompromising war on evil. Actually, dualism turns evil into a metaphysical principle, equal ultimately with

[16] Barth himself resorts to it (1956: 493).

good. Dualism grants evil a place with good, within some kind of order. Indignation at its presence thus becomes pointless. Berkouwer (1971: 70) makes the incisive comment: 'Dualism is only a cosmic excuse in metaphysical garb.' But sin in experience and in the doctrine of original sin is literally *atopos* – a word used in the New Testament for people who behave 'out of order', with malignant motives (2 Thes. 3:2).[17]

In line with this, I wonder whether the category of *accident* is perfectly adequate for sin. Turretin (1847: 575 [IX.11.2–3]), who follows the scholastic tradition, calls sin an 'accident' in order rightly to oppose Matthias Flacius Illyricus' misunderstanding that sin should be considered as a substance. But 'accident' may say too little (that was indeed Flacius' concern, and also C. S. Lewis's when he used the language criticized earlier). It may also suggest the application of a scheme drawn from the good order of God's creation – the created distinction between substance and accident – while sin is no *mere* accident like the other accidents in substances. Sin is a unique alteration – not even *sui generis,* for it does not constitute a *genus*, a lawful compartment within order! Sin affects created being more deeply, pervasively and destructively than any accident; and yet it has no substantial reality. It 'is' nothing in itself, but perversion, corruption, abuse and misuse of the good.

Shared inheritance and individual decision

In the Germanic languages, original sin is called *hereditary* sin (German *Erbsünde*). As part of this survey of human experience for evidence relevant to our doctrine, we should enquire about such aspects as would correspond to the combination, in the doctrine of original sin, of heredity and personal responsibility.

---

[17] Gesché (1993: 53 and 105 n. 6) refers to Kant for the thought that Christianity repelled Gnostic dualism in locating evil in a *third* place, hell, beside heaven and earth. Kant's actual meaning is unclear; Kant 1960: 53n. emphasizes that good men and evil are completely dissimilar, separated by an 'immeasurable gulf'. I would comment further that hell is not the location of evil (not the realm of the devil) in the biblical view, but the place of righteousness vindicated, holiness glorified, rebels reconciled in the sense of Col. 1:20. Evil owns no place at all.

The starting-point, the riddle, is found in the entanglement of social factors and individual spontaneity in the common experience of evil. For centuries, or millennia, no-one doubted that misconduct was to be blamed on, and chastized in the person of, the subject. We moderns, however, have grown more and more conscious of the social 'conditioning' of individual behaviour – to the extent that behaviour may appear, in deterministic fashion, to be the mere result of objective factors and of their interplay. Comparative statistics suggest it. The scientific approach, which tends to reduce its object to a causal nexus (or a nexus of regularities), undergirds the view. Anthropology has revealed how the symbolic systems of our cultures, and especially language, mould us and impregnate our deepest convictions and sensitivities; anthropology sees the individual as the expression of his or her symbolic world. Even morally, solidarity as a value seems to receive due homage in the new perspective, which is so diametrically opposed to Pharisaic isolation (Lk. 18:11). The net result is that individual responsibility almost vanishes.

But it cannot vanish. The sense of free agency, of being the source of one's actions through personal choice, is also a fact of experience.[18] We cannot repress it. Modern individualism actually heightens this sense to an extreme degree. We are caught between the tide of determinism and the cult of the autonomous self.

In order to relieve the tension, some criticize on epistemological grounds the unwarranted 'reductionism' often associated with scientific method. Human being transcends what 'controlling knowledge' can apprehend; experience witnesses, for those who have ears to hear, to the mystery of humanness, to the human person as *homo absconditus* (whether there be a 'hidden God' or not). Some refuse to exploit anthropology for ideological ends; recent trends are moving away from the pan-cultural, pan-linguistic, creed.[19] Such helpful considerations, however, lack the power to heal the contradiction. Most people appear to live with the tension between a deterministic social

---

[18] Pannenberg (1994: 256) firmly maintains that 'Only with the consent of the individual will does the evil influence of society become the sin of the individual.'

[19] So says a prestigious scholar in the field, Marcel Gauchet (1993: 18).

model and their affirmation of individual freedom: two poles of a lazy dialectic they cannot solve and choose to put to the back of their minds.

I suggest that the duality of experience is better explained by the doctrine of original sin. It teaches both personal responsibility ('I am a man of unclean lips') and social conditioning and solidarity ('and I dwell among a people of unclean lips'; Is. 6:5). But the tension is not unbearable because the biblical view does not absolutize any of the terms. Under the authority of the creator God, causal (scientific) determinations cannot be ultimate; they cannot stifle the mystery of the 'divine image'. Under the authority of the creator God, personal freedom cannot exist of itself, but only as a gift, in theonomous (not autonomous) relationship. Thus, and thus only, is there room for both, and both can be held together.

At any rate, one cannot deny a congruity between the 'riddle' of experience and the tenets of our doctrine: sin is of the race, and at the same time it is of each one of us because each of us wills to sin.

Alongside the 'synchronic' viewpoint (seeing humankind at one particular point in time), we must place the 'diachronic' perspective of chronological succession. Experience finds evil not only around us, but *before* us. We are born into a situation in which evil abounds. There is a tradition of evil which informs us, or deforms us, and which we appropriate by our own initiatives. Few would dispute that human experience thus corresponds roughly and formally with the two elements in the German term *Erb/sünde*.

From inheritance to heredity, however (in spite of etymology), there is a distinct step. Among scientists, controversy has raged for decades: if the debate over innate and acquired traits has seen a rehabilitation of heredity (genetic determination), the true solution seems to be that personal behaviour results from an infinitely complex interaction. Empirical data from daily life include the beginnings of evil – pride and greed, deceit and cruelty – at the earliest age. Children are like their parents in temperament, in intellectual and other gifts (think of the Bach family!), and even in moral traits. But this is by no means uniform and automatic, and we cling to the immediate 'feeling' that each person chooses individually either to adopt or reject family mores.

Does the doctrine of original sin illuminate this facet of the riddle? Simply to answer 'yes', admittedly, would be to claim too much too soon, inasmuch as the heredity of original sin remains the most obscure element in the doctrine; it calls for more cautious efforts at clarification. Yet we may notice how faithfully the combination in the doctrine fits the duality in experience. This is biblical realism.

Our investigation must look beyond family resemblance and social solidarity to wider horizons. The universal sway of evil influence is a most impressive datum. It is the grim face, the wrong side, of an essential and striking feature of human life: the unity of our race. Pierre Teilhard de Chardin highlights the contrast with animal evolution: whereas all other species tend to diverge, the boughs of humankind tend to converge and coalesce.[20] This was true throughout history, but it has become obvious to us. For the first time, all peoples on earth tend to adopt the same basic 'way of life', with astonishing conformity of dress, taste and aspirations among youth everywhere. And everywhere, similar unrest and crime, egoism and unbridled lust are evident. 'The whole world lies in [the power of] the evil one' (1 Jn. 5:19).

Adam's role in biblical doctrine throws remarkable light on the 'empirical' fact of human universality. Not only does Scripture stress the unity of the race, based on a common origin (Acts 17:26; cf. Gn. 3:20), but it conceives of groups, and ultimately of humankind, as organic wholes under representative 'heads'. Communities are more than aggregates of individuals; they have an identity of their own, which is expressed in the person of the leader. Scholars of a former generation had an inkling of that structure, which they labelled 'corporate personality'; but they considered it more a mode of 'Hebrew thinking' than an account of ontological truth. They ascribed to the so-called Hebrew mind a fuzzy identification of individuality and belonging, seeming to delight in such a purported loss of distinctions. In that mid-twentieth-century

---

[20] *E.g.* Teilhard 1962: 106ff., or 1955: 267ff. and earlier 194f., 230ff. Teilhard was wont to repeat his propositions: 'One could almost say', Claude Tresmontant (1956: 11) once observed, 'that Teilhard did not write two hundred essays, but rather that he started again two hundred times on the same essay, to his last day.'

form, the theory has been rightly branded as an academic 'myth'.[21] We now prefer to speak of 'headship', without prejudice to individuality. Contrary to animal species, the human race is one in some spiritual way, as well as genetically; it is furnished with a 'head'. We could say, to borrow a term from botany, that it is 'capitate' – hence the phrases 'in Adam' and 'in Christ', Christ being the Head in the new creation of our kind. From this derives the apostle's emphasis that the human 'image' we bear is defined in the first or in the second man (1 Cor. 15:48f.).

The structure of racial headship exposes the misleading excesses in Kierkegaard's dialectic of race and individual. He does not entrench himself at either pole: 'At every moment,' he stresses, 'the individual is both himself and the race' (1980: 28). Both terms tend to be absolutized unduly. Human nature is made excessively one, like a Platonic 'idea', and is considered to be entirely present in any one individual. Conversely, each individual, endowed with freedom, is excessively autonomous, for 'freedom is infinite and arises out of nothing' (p. 112). Instead of the complex and balanced headship structure, which holds together by virtue of God's foundational authority, a contradiction or antinomy is introduced, and this generates a pattern of thinking in paradoxes. But the moderate scheme the present study has detected in Scripture is truer to experience than these dazzling flashes of paradox.

It is worth noting that C. S. Lewis (1940: 75) came very close to this understanding of racial headship. He suggested that in Adam and in Christ

> ... the separateness – modified only by causal relations – which we discern between individuals, is balanced, in absolute reality, by some kind of 'inter-animation' of which we have no conception at all. It

---

[21] See the powerful attack mounted by Stanley E. Porter (1990b: 289ff., esp. 291–298). H. Wheeler Robinson was the main pioneer of the 'corporate personality' line, and there was an alliance with the Pedersen-Boman development on the alleged originality of the Hebrew mind (the 'myth' which James Barr exploded). On corporate personality, the earlier critics were J. R. Porter 1965 and Rogerson 1970.

may be that the acts and sufferings of great archetypal individuals such as Adam and Christ are ours, not by legal fiction, metaphor, or causality, but in some much deeper fashion. There is no question, of course, of individuals melting down into a kind of spiritual continuum such as Pantheistic systems believe in; that is excluded by the whole tenor of our faith. But there may be a tension between individuality and some other principle.

There is enough evidence in the way human life actually functions to warrant this hypothesis.

An additional comment could be made on the structure which binds the spiritual oneness of humankind while maintaining individual distinction. It may belong to the reflections or traces of the Trinity one can find in creation (*vestigia trinitatis*). As one climbs the scale of created being, individual distinction and unity grow together – pointing, perhaps, to the mystery of the absolute distinction of the Three within the absolute unity of the one divine essence. Take a stone: it is one, but poorly and weakly so; conversely, its component parts are little differentiated, and their individuality is low. Take an animal: the organic oneness it shows is clearly richer; at the same time, its members are more specialized or individualized. Take the human person, the human spirit: a higher degree of unity is reached, which enables the person to say 'I' (the condition of spirituality); but it is also more complex, with a marked distinction between intelligence and will (by contrast with animal instinct, which resembles an obscure blend of the two). The higher the creature, the stronger both these traits become. This increase of individualization within increasing unity can be seen from the 'collective' angle as well. Take a heap of stones: its unity is minimal, as is also the individuality of each stone. Take an animal species: it enjoys an obvious unity (genetic, biological, ecological), while each member of the species, this cat or this dog, possesses a significant individuality. With humankind, however, the individuality of the members of the species becomes a major feature, both for ontology and for ethics; at the same time, communities (the sexual pair, to begin with) are called to achieve a deeper, richer and stronger kind of unity. In harmony with this vision,

ORIGINAL SIN AS A KEY TO HUMAN EXPERIENCE

the spiritual unity of our race under one head should not appear so strange to our contemplation.[22]

Necessity and responsibility

Even theologians who wander far from the Augustinian path sometimes praise the doctrine for attempting to combine fate and guilt – as does Dorothee Sölle, who is among those who wander the farthest.[23] Is the confrontation with human experience, generally, instructive on this point also?

While very few would be ready to reject the belief that sin is rooted in the free agency of individuals, few would deny that there is also an element of necessity. Human experience of evil invites such a thought in two ways, at least. First, the universal sway evil holds in the world suggests that it is *inescapable*: if all do it – *cosi fan tutte* – some necessity must be operating. Secondly, the *compulsive* power one can feel in the process of temptation constitutes a primary datum. Who may pretend to be entirely free? Jesus' word pierces all illusions: 'Everyone who commits sin is a slave' (Jn. 8:34). Paul's desperate description of the struggle between the 'law of his mind' and the law he finds in his 'members' illustrates the bondage of sin (Rom. 7:14–24). Ovid's oft-quoted verse which confesses that he sees and approves the better things, yet actually follows the worse (*Video meliora proboque, deteriora sequor*), shows that some awareness of that serfdom exists outside special revelation.

This is certainly a 'riddle'. And the terms of the riddle correspond to the tenets of the church's doctrine. Turretin laboured to maintain both the necessity and the voluntary character of (originated) original sin: 'What is necessary of physical necessity or because of coercion cannot be considered as sin; but, regularly, what is necessary of hypothetical and rational necessity does not remove the character of sin' (1847:

[22] This is a development of insights found among Roman Catholic theologians. The earliest occurrence I have met is in Henri de Lubac (1947: 285)', who himself refers to a 1917 article by Teilhard.

[23] Ted Peters (1994: 30 n. 24) writes: 'Dorothee Sölle argues that the doctrine of original sin maintains an important dialectic between fate and guilt.'

538 [IX.3.10]).[24] Reinhold Niebuhr (1941: 251ff.) substituted 'inevitability' for 'necessity', but this 'paradox' simply expresses the riddle once more with another word.

Kierkegaard, while criticizing original sin as a false interpretation of this necessity, seemed to acknowledge both the necessity and the guilt. For him, since the Christian concept of sin and guilt posits the individual, 'the point is only that he is guilty, and yet he is supposed to have become guilty by fate . . .' (1980: 98).[25] In spite of the 'qualitative leap', Kierkegaard describes anxiety giving birth, as it were inevitably, to transgression, which means preferring the finite over the infinite: 'Here anxiety is the dizziness of freedom, which emerges when the spirit wants to posit the synthesis [of soul and body] and freedom looks down into its own possibility, laying hold of finiteness to support itself' (p. 61).[26] When freedom raises its head, he says, it is guilty. After Adam, there is a 'quantitative' increase which creates an even stronger impression of guilt arising from anxiety alone (p. 53), and 'sensuousness is constantly degraded to mean sinfulness' (p. 58).[27] These elements in his thought establish that Kierkegaard also combined some degree of necessity with his passion for infinite freedom.

Church doctrine agrees with experience when it links universal compulsion and personal responsibility for misdeeds – involving freedom in some sense. But here lies the greatest difficulty. How can both coexist? The doctrine faces the issue boldly, and claims to show how it is possible for the bondage of all human beings from birth to be attributed to the will – and not be included in the metaphysical definition of humanness. It does so, as became clear in our discussion of the interpretation of Genesis 3, by pointing to the *historical* character of original sin. Humankind, as represented by its head, fell because of a

[24] 'Quod est necessarium necessitate physica, vel coactionis, non potest habere rationem peccati; sed quod est necessarium necessitate hypothetica et rationali, non statim tollit peccatum.' *Cf.* para. 9, same page.

[25] The French translation (by Knud Ferlov and Jean-J. Gateau) does not include the equivalent of the words 'is supposed to'.

[26] On this delicate issue, *cf.* Kierkegaard's p. 49, where he stresses that anxiety is not a category of necessity, or of freedom; 'it is entangled freedom'.

[27] *Cf.* p. 63. In this connection, we must remember that 'the ultimate point of the sensuous is precisely the sexual' (p. 49), and that it is also the temporal: 'The moment sin is posited, temporality is sinfulness' (p. 92).

misuse of freedom. As stemming from Adam, original sin is truly sin, the guilty distortion of God's gifts; it is not to be confused with being finite, or earthly, or imperfectly evolved. Sin's historical origin makes it a matter of tragic necessity, but not of fate.[28] This was the position defended in that discussion, agreeing with Schönborn and even Williams, against the objections of writers such as Brunner and Ricœur.

If we again appeal to 'experience', we receive some support, or at least some comfort, from unexpected quarters. The power of the biblical insight seems to have touched some non-Christian thinkers; they cannot help positing something like a primeval fall. The most notable example would be the Freudian one: in spite of criticisms, Freud clung to the 'myth' he had constructed – of the original murder of the horde's chief by his sons and their incest with the mothers – and which he intended as historical truth. He did so strenuously, and, indeed, wisely, for his superior genius sensed that the private 'Oedipus' of each individual was not enough to account for the phenomenon of history, for the plight of humankind.[29] René Girard built an alternative scheme, though the collective murder of the unfortunate 'scapegoat' man is, to him, *the* source of culture.[30] The Marxist story offers parallel suggestions, though fraught with ambiguity: primitive accumulation and the first division of labour resemble a fall from the 'golden' state of perfect equality and community of goods, with every task (including surplus value) one with the individual who performed it. Yet the earlier state is also that of unmediated subjection to nature, in utter human helplessness; the fall is, in Hegelian fashion, a fall 'upwards'.[31] The most

---

[28] Turretin (1847: 573 [IX.10.15]) writes of sin: 'Non sit voluntarium *actu*, est tamen *ortu*; *voluntate* ejus *a quo* est, etsi non proprie *voluntate* ejus *in quo* est . . .' ('It is not voluntary by virtue of the act, but by virtue of its origin; by the will of him from whom it proceeds, even if, strictly, it is not by the will of him in whom it is found'). He goes on, of course, to stress that it *inheres* in the sinner's will and is also voluntary because of that.

[29] The depth and validity of Freud's insight have been shown by Jacques Gagey 1982, especially ch. 6, mainly on *Totem and Taboo* (pp. 158ff.). *Cf.* ch. 7, mainly on the second 'myth', that of *Moses and Monotheism*.

[30] I refer to the main exposition of his thought, Girard 1978.

[31] This is the way to reconcile apparent divergencies. In the light of some statements, Gary North (1968: 92) rightly insists that 'Marx *did* share with the

surprising witness comes from Jean-Paul Sartre, of all philosophers. He was able to discern that 'Man is a being to whom something happened'.[32]

One should notice that the doctrine of original sin not only 'protects' guilt or responsibility from its denial under the crushing impression of necessity; it also mitigates what could become inordinate harshness. The bondage of the will of the race considered as an organic whole allows for a humane measure in indictment. The idea of a humane measure is biblical; the Lord tells David that he will chastise his disobedient sons 'with the rod of humans and with the blows of Adam's sons' (2 Sa. 7:14). Pelagius' severity is unbearable, as Williams (1927: 357) remarked. Absolute freedom entails absolute condemnation; optimism turns to rigorism. It is Adolphe Gesché's strongest theme that our generation is oppressed by 'hyper-responsibility' and 'over-guilt', and should welcome the doctrine of original sin as the good news of a more humane evaluation (1993: 40, 54, 63ff., 81f., 107f., 115, 135f.). He may be right in his diagnosis – under the guise of permissiveness and relativism, their opposite lies in hidden, repressed form – and we should certainly hear his call for a sober confession of sin (pp. 136, 141). Dostoevsky's hero exclaims, 'I am guilty of everything, before all and towards all', but this is false humility. We should rather follow Chancellor Jehan Gerson (1363–1429) who has Satan saying to the dying man, 'I tell you you shall be damned', and the man rightly replying, 'You are not the judge, but only the

---

ancients a belief in a past Golden Age', as evidenced in his *Grundrisse,* Friedrich Engels' *Origin of the Family, Private Property and the State* unfolds this conviction. But, at the same time, as Kostas Papaïoannou (1972: 68f.) clarifies, humankind's primitive relationship to nature is severely limited, very near to that deadening idolatry which Marx thoroughly despised. Hence Engels can use the word 'fall' and add that it was a step forward (p. 69). Regarding 'primitive accumulation' in the special form that made capitalism possible, Jean-Yves Calvez (1970: 188) uses the phrase 'a kind of economic original sin'. Nicolas Berdyaev wrote: 'Marx's belief in exploitation, as the fundamental and determinative fact of social life, may be assimilated to the Christian doctrine of original sin', as quoted from his *Le Marxisme et la religion,* in Berdyaev 1975: 55 n. 8.

[32] Sartre, *Cahiers pour une morale* (Paris, 1983), p. 51, as quoted by Gesché 1993: 49.

slanderer. You are the damned one, not the one who can condemn.'[33]

In order more deeply to pursue our reflection on the conjunction of event and permanent state, or disposition (*habitus*) – of necessity attached to nature, and voluntary orientation – we should have to consider the underlying structure of created time. We should perceive that the foundation of continuities and singularities in the sovereign Lord's design ('He works out all things according to the plan he has decided', Eph. 1:11) allows for both without erecting an ultimate antinomy. On the contrary, the idolatry of time, historicism, destroys history by crushing it and blowing it away like dust. Oliver O'Donovan (1986: 60) vigorously makes the point:

> When history is made the categorical matrix for all meaning and value, it cannot then be taken seriously *as history* . . . when that world is itself dissolved into history, as all the characters of Joyce's *Finnegan's Wake* are dissolved into prose, then history is left without a subject, so we have no history any more . . .

The converse absolutization, the denial of time as real, also loses history by freezing it as metaphysics.

Fleshing out the bones of this most difficult topic of time would require a discussion far beyond the scope of this study and of the available resources. Suffice it to say that in the perspective of Scripture, we have been given a nature, a metaphysical definition, that is truly engaged in history; it is affected, but not exhausted, by what happens, through the exercise of created freedom. We are thus subjects in history. This structure made it possible for the Adamic event to produce a non-metaphysical corruption of nature – original sin.

It also rendered possible the counter-move, historical redemption. Of this, more later.

---

[33] Gesché 1993: 141, with n. 15 referring to M.-J. Pinet, *La Vie ardente de Gerson* (Paris: 1929), p. 142.

Chapter Five

Original sin as propagated and broken

We cannot avoid facing the riddle of original sin itself. We have observed that the doctrine, as stated and unfolded, sheds light on the human predicament. It corresponds to our universal experience, and better enables us to discern and recognize life's enigmas as we deal with (or name) their elements in a balanced way. We understand them more intelligently, and with a unique realism, when we apply the grid of 'original sin' in a biblical sense. This was (though he used other terms) Pascal's argument, and the previous chapter contended that universal experience substantiates the claim. But what if the doctrine itself remains opaque? If it consists of nothing but absurdity, sophistry, a monstrous mixture of incompatible themes (as some would charge), is the profit worth the price? Can we in all honesty pay that price, thus 'sacrificing our intellect'? Is there indeed any profit left, beyond mere illusion?

I hope to show that an orthodox theologian's situation is far less precarious than these (somewhat rhetorical) questions may suggest, and that the difficulty of the riddle is at least bearable and instructive. While there is no magical solution waiting to be pulled out of a hat, I shall offer considerations which have proved helpful to some, and may so prove to others. Several of them were introduced in previous chapters; I shall appeal to them again, and add a few more.

Undoubtedly, the Augustinian doctrine of original sin has aroused vehement and passionate reactions down to the present. Many believers as well as unbelievers – even famous thinkers of the church – have found its core affirmations preposterous. Williams, undeterred by English academic courtesy, heaps on Augustine's arguments such descriptions as 'abstruse', 'macabre', 'gloomy', 'worthless from the point of view of modern thought', and marred by 'fanatical logic' (1927: 369, 372f., 380, 377). The commonest objection may be the strongest one: if I have been a guilty and condemned sinner since I was in my mother's womb, because of Adam's misuse of his freedom, *it is not fair!*[1] The more refined version concentrates on the combination of two different languages when the propagation of original sin is explained or defined. Kierkegaard's critical acumen touched the sorest nerve: original sin, he said, 'combines categories "qualitatively heterogeneous". To inherit is a "category of nature", offence is an "ethical category of the spirit".'[2] Williams (1927: 296) comments on Cyprian's views that he 'oscillates illogically between what has been called the medical and the forensic ways of regarding sin; but such a confusion . . . is inherent in the idea of Original Guilt'.[3] Paul Ricœur phrases the charge in more biting words: an 'inconsistent notion', a 'pseudo-concept', parading 'false knowledge', confuses the biological and the juridical (1974c: 270, 280, 285; 1974b: 305). This is why Karl Barth, as we saw, could accept the phrase 'original sin' (*peccatum originale, Ursünde*) when provided with a Christological foundation, while he could not accept the usual German term, *Erbsünde*, 'hereditary sin' (1956: 500 [para. 60/3]).

This final chapter, while attempting to gather together our findings in a more systematic form, will be concerned centrally with the issue of 'propagation', of humankind's universal involvement in sin 'because' Adam, in Eden's beginning, disobeyed. A preliminary move will set aside the 'facile' solution of irrationality. I shall then survey traditional ways of relieving

[1] See, *e.g.*, Moo 1991: 339, with a quotation from Pannenberg (n. 41) who reacts with a violent 'impossible' verdict (in his *Anthropology*, p. 124). Pannenberg is more restrained when writing elsewhere, but he nevertheless considers the ascription of *guilt* to be 'incompatible' with sin as a state and a bondage: 'Incompatible [with the application of the theme of guilt], however, is the state of the wicked heart or of rebellion against God as the background of individual actions, or as the Pauline concept [of sin] as a power that rules and indwells us' (1994: 261).

[2] Quoted in Viallaneix 1979: 72 from Kierkegaard's *Papirer* (*Journals*) 10 (2) A. 481. But Kierkegaard added immediately: 'Here we must believe' (*ibid.*); he seems to express more sympathy for the church doctrine in this discussion than he does in *The Concept of Anxiety*, and he rather approves of the logical incongruity which he calls 'paradox'.

[3] *Cf.* Emil Brunner (1947: 143), who rejects what the doctrine states: '. . . the responsible act of an individual, whose guilt, for incomprehensible reasons, is fastened on us, and whose sin is transferred to us in a manner which is quite incompatible with the nature of sin, namely, through natural inheritance.'

the tension; without despising the help they offer, I conclude that they fall short of an adequate explanation. I therefore seek to strengthen and complement them, and hope to achieve a viable account of the matter (drawing on the conclusions of chapter 3). Ultimately, I sketch the *positive* perspective which the doctrine of original sin opens up when it is heartily embraced and understood.

No refuge in unreason

Renouncing the idea that sinfulness stems from a definite historical origin and thereafter is transmitted, merely to keep the paradox of bondage and guilt intertwined in glorious irrationality, is not an option. Despite the weight of such impressive names as Brunner, Niebuhr and Ricœur, this (pseudo)solution cannot be maintained with evangelical consistency. It conflicts, as I have shown, with the teaching of Scripture. It ignores some elements in experience. It slips back, in open or hidden fashion, into metaphysical interpretations of evil. It is not a road we should travel.

There is another way, however, to invoke irrationality when the difficulty of the propagation of original sin is raised. While holding fast to the doctrine, including the starting-point in time and space, it is possible to conclude that the riddle cannot be solved, and, then, to justify the theologians' failure by pointing to the irrational character of sin anyway – an offence to reason. Berkouwer (1971: 512ff.), after patiently reviewing Pelagian, Augustinian and Reformed federalist views, and having found them wanting, shows himself sympathetic to suggestions of 'corporate personality', but nevertheless wisely notes that the phrase 'cannot be taken as a magic formula or a panacea' (p. 532).[4] Ultimately, he rejoices that no rational explanation of the spread of sin can be found; an explanation, he argues, would lead to self-excuse and would smack of fatalism (p. 523). Moo (1991: 340f.) seems to settle for a similar stance as he remembers Pascal's emphasis that the doctrine is incomprehensible.[5]

---

[4] He also criticizes some writers (p. 515) for their amalgam of causality and 'corporate personality' categories.

[5] 'No explanation ultimately removes the problem', '. . . offense to reason'.

This strategy is not lacking in appeal. When no adequate solution is forthcoming, it is braver and wiser to acknowledge the fact than to hide behind a smokescreen of dubious arguments. More important still; the radical, irredeemable, irrationality of sin *is* a decisive truth. My earlier (1994) investigation of the ultimate origin of evil led to a demonstration of exactly that thesis: no rational explanation was ever offered, nor should any be sought, in the light of Scripture. Among our spiritual forebears we have to deplore a strange deficit of sensitivity regarding this major issue. When the great Turretin argues that 'we should not wonder if man, who was created a fallible and changeable being, should have changed and fallen',[6] where is the prophet's burning indignation, where is the apostle's horror of sin? Along similar lines, John H. Gerstner chides Jonathan Edwards for rationally deriving human sin from mere imperfection: 'It was not unthinkable to Jonathan Edwards that God could have created man with "a fixed prevailing principle of sin in his heart". That is apparently the imperfection that is native to the moral creature.'[7]

Kierkegaard's insight, on the contrary, brings out the awful unreason of sin's emergence, which implies the opaque mystery of its being granted permission by the sovereign Holy One. He wrote in the *Journals*: 'Sin is precisely what cannot be conceived of and penetrated, the riddle of the world, because it is the groundless thing, a gratuitous interruption.'[8] He also noted, we should remember, that sin cannot be located in any place proper to itself, and that it is defined by that oddity (1980: 14).[9] Sin is *atopos* and a *skandalon*.

It is not self-evident, however, that what is true of sin entering into the world, arising in its qualitative difference, extends to the spread or propagation of sin. The leap here is unwarranted. Nothing can explain or excuse the contingent event of the first abuse of freedom, but the consequences were not *so* unexpected. The man, who was upright, 'blameless since the day of [his] creation' (Ezk. 28:15), who delighted continually in the

[6] Turretin 1847: 550 [IX.7.6]: 'Nec mirum videri debet, si homo qui labilis et mutabilis conditus erat, mutatus sit et lapsus . . .'
[7] Gerstner 1992: 310; *cf.* 318f. with a full quotation and the reference to the Yale edition of Edwards' *Works* I: 413.
[8] Kierkegaard, *Papirer* 10 (2) A. 436, as quoted by Viallaneix 1979: 71.
[9] *Cf.* n. 43 in chapter 2 above, where the same reference was cited.

presence of God and of Wisdom (Pr. 8:31), who was bathed in the sunshine of God's blessing and always responded in trust and gratitude – that man rebelled. This is opaque, absurd and unexplained; but what followed seems to have done so rather logically.

Several traits suggest that the spread of sin occurred along rational lines – forbidding us to take refuge in unreason. Universality, constancy and necessity belong to the characteristics of that process, and they savour of rationality. If, after Adam, all people are born sinners, we may not simply say, 'It just happens; there is no reason.' Sin, being corruption, perversion, constantly uses created reality as a tool and vehicle through the variety of its manifestations. It must have employed some cause, law or structure of creation in order to spread from Adam to all.

Berkouwer's conclusion that there is no rational explanation is linked to slight deficiencies in his handling of relevant passages and to his misguided efforts at eliminating the very idea of propagation.[10] His sympathy with a milder form of irrationalism may have seduced him into an ill-advised strategy.

Traditional metaphors

The time-honoured strategy of most Augustinian theologians has been to draw on the resources of language. Traditional attempts at explanation have resorted to metaphor, with undeniable effect; many have found such schemes illuminating. But there has been little analytical rigour; indeed, it is not certain that those who devised the schemes were fully aware of their metaphorical status.

Caution is necessary when dealing with figures of speech. In a way, the whole of language is based on metaphors. Yet we should distinguish between living metaphors, for which the distance between the two referents A and B is preserved in the implied comparison of A and B (the distance signified by the *meta* in 'metaphor'), and dead metaphors, which are so worn out by common use that they are now used directly to predicate B as a

---

[10] Berkouwer (1971: 532) speaks of propagation as 'congenial to fatalism but never to man's *guilt*'. Passages such as Job 14:4; Jn. 3:5f.; Ps. 51:5, merely point to the universal sinfulness of humankind (pp. 488f.; he deliberately ignores the emphasis on birth or provenance in these texts). Paul's interest in Rom. 5, he writes, is only in grace and Christ (pp. 496, 510).

quality of *A*. In living metaphors, an uncertain resemblance connects *A* and *B* across the distance: the phrase 'the fires of passion' implies the distinct reality of both fire and passion, while indicating similarities between the two. In dead metaphors one thinks of *A* only under a *B* aspect, of *A(B)*, as in 'St Anthony's fire', where 'fire' refers to a particular kind of inflammation. We may conjecture intermediate uses and forces, however, when degrees of distance are still present. Needless to say, it is necessary to discern the kind or level of metaphorical talk in order more accurately to appreciate its contribution to knowledge and theory.

The master metaphor, in the doctrine of original sin, has been drawn from medicine and genetics. Starting with *4 Ezra*'s *permanens infirmitas* (3:21f.) and Tertullian's *vitium originis*,[11] theologians have spoken of original sin as an infection, an infirmity, and thus a contagious alteration of human nature. After Anselm's 'lepers beget lepers, thus our first parents', Luther could tell of the 'sickness of a nature vitiated by sin'.[12] The Augsburg Confession (art. 2) describes original sin as an 'inborn disease'.[13] Among modern theologians, reference was made earlier to Bernard Ramm, who reads the medical metaphor into Romans 5,[14] and to David L. Smith (1994: 369, 371; quoted above, ch. 1, p. 31), who goes farther, and insistently compares original sin to a virus transmitted from parents to children, like HIV, or to a genetic disease.

The metaphor looks very apt: just like hereditary sickness, sin is an incapacitating alteration of nature, which was once contracted in the genealogical line and goes on being transmitted; it produces uncleanness and leads to death.

Yet this very attractiveness may be seductive. We are in

[11] Williams 1927: 245, quoting from Tertullian's *De anima* 41.

[12] Brunner 1947: 121 n. 2, quoting from Anselm's *De conceptu virginali* . . . 2 ('ex parentibus leprosis generantur leprosi, ita ex primis parentibus', see above, chapter 1 n. 36), and 138 n. 1, from Luther's *Werke, Weimar Ausgabe* 42, 433; 'observamus, quod inter morbum naturae per peccatum vitiatae, et suum opus . . . spiritus sanctus discernit . . .'; 'we observe that between the sickness of a nature vitiated by sin, and his work, the Holy Spirit discerns . . .'

[13] In German, *angeborne Seuch*, and *morbus* in Latin.

[14] See above, chapter 3, p. 66, quoting from Ramm 1985: 56: 'Sin is not seen so much as a formal breaking of a specified law but as a contagious disease that spreads through a population.' On p. 57, he writes that humankind is 'sinful *genetically*', but not in a precise, technical, sense (as it appears).

danger of losing sight of the metaphorical distance (between *A* and *B*, between sin and sickness), and this danger, history shows, is not imaginary. Sin may be similar to a genetic disease, but *it is not one.* Hughes (1989: 131) is helpfully firm here, and Kierkegaard's (1980: 15) strident protest against the distortion of the concept of sin still resounds: 'Whenever sin is spoken of as a disease, an abnormality, a poison, or a disharmony, the concept is falsified.' We must not disregard the radical 'qualitative difference'. The whole difficulty of the spread of sin through the generations is that it involves voluntary disposition (wilful intent) and responsibility – which amount to guilt – whereas sickness, even when psychological, does not. The metaphor may be deceptively glossing over the crucial point.

Scripture does not ignore the 'medical' metaphor. Jeremiah, when he laments the heart's perversity, describes it as *'ānuš,* which the New English Bible renders 'desperately sick' (Je. 17:9). The apostle refers to our sinful state with the word *asthenēs,* which has connotations not only of weakness but also of illness (Rom. 5:6). Hebrew poetic parallelism associates disease and sins: 'No-one living in Zion will say, "I am ill"; and the sins of those who dwell there will be forgiven' (Is. 33:24, NIV).[15] Our Lord himself referred to the righteous and sinners as 'the healthy' and 'the sick' (Mt. 9:12f.), and various diseases (palsy, blindness, leprosy) have a symbolic value in the gospel stories of his healings. They may have had the same value, according to the divine intention, in the Old Testament purity laws. Yet, on the whole, the restraint of Scripture contrasts with the massive confidence of many in the explanatory power of the sickness metaphor: it is as if Scripture *avoided* putting forward the metaphor in attempts to account for the transmission of sin.

Traditional theology has closely bound another motif to the metaphor of sickness. Throughout the history of the doctrine, we can detect the lurking sentiment that the way human beings come into existence, the *sexual* way, cannot but vitiate their nature. 'Without this element,' Brunner writes, 'the doctrine of Original Sin is inconceivable' (1947: 121 n. 2). Augustine

---

[15] We should not quote Is. 1:5ff., however, since the metaphor in that passage illustrates the effects of divine punishment rather than sin itself.

emphasized the connection, though he had to face the Pelagian charge that the idea was a Manichean residue and though he maintained, in full consistency with his theology of creation, that sex had been created good. 'There is no doubt that Augustine associates the transmission of "original sin" with *libido*, particularly displayed in the autonomous action and sensation of the genitals, especially the male genitals' (Rist 1994: 319).[16] His concern seems to have been our inability to control our own bodies – a penal effect of the fall, and a harbinger of death, the final separation of soul and body (pp. 321, 324).[17]

Augustine was not the first to be suspicious of the role of sexuality. Williams (1927: 57f., 122) makes much of the presence in Judaism of the theme of Eve's sexual 'defilement' (*inquinamentum*), by the serpent, which polluted her posterity; he sees cursory allusions to that theme in 2 Corinthians 11:3 and 1 Timothy 2:14. In his view, Clement of Alexandria probably interpreted the sin of Genesis 3 as premature sex, with some causal connection with our lusts (pp. 204f., based on the *Stromata* III.xv.94), and Gregory of Nyssa taught that sex was added *in view of the fall* which was foreseen (p. 272). Nearer to Augustine, Ambrose was afflicted with a true phobia of sex (p. 304). Williams finds a trace of the same connection even in Thomas Aquinas's treatise *On Evil*: 'Through the defect of bodily semen, the generative force transmits original sin together with human nature' (p. 403 n. 2).[18] Turretin is able to speak of 'impure generation', although the sexual reference is not certain (1847: 578 [IX.12.2]).[19] Kierkegaard, in his own way, tightly bound sinfulness (peccability) together with sensuousness and sexuality; as soon as sin is there, sensuousness is degraded into sinfulness, and 'the ultimate point of the

[16] Rist's two appendixes, 1994: 317–327, offer a model treatment of Augustine's exact position.

[17] Julian of Eclanum did not understand Augustine's problem (Rist 1994: 326f.).

[18] Quoting from *De malo* iv.2: 'Vis generativa per decisionem corporalis seminis operatur ad traductionem peccati originalis simul cum natura humana.' The difficult word is *decisio*, which may mean 'decrease' or 'arrangement', and which I venture to render 'defect'.

[19] '*Generalius*, modum propagationis istius esse *impuram generationem*, qua ex corruptis et peccatoribus corrupti et peccatores nascimur' ('*More generally*, the mode of this propagation is *unclean generation*, by which we are born corrupt and sinful people of corrupt and sinful parents').

sensuous is precisely the sexual' (1980: 58f., 49).[20] 'A perfect spirit cannot be conceived as sexually qualified', and 'the sexual difference as a drive' entered into the world with sin – 'without sin there is no sexuality' (pp. 79, 76, 49).[21] The young man whose education led him to identify sensuousness and sinfulness should probably be understood as a self-portrait (p. 75).[22]

It would be facile, and, indeed, unworthy, to discard the connection as the symptom of Augustine's and Kierkegaard's personal problems. The fascinating power of the supposed link through the centuries calls for a deeper evaluation. With sober competence, Pannenberg (1994: 242) criticizes the many who 'have overhastily dismissed Augustine's teaching' on concupiscence.[23] Peters (1994: 140) courageously unmasks the motive of several critics: 'Foes of . . . traditional morality in our own generation have indulged in a good deal of Augustine bashing as they have pressed their point of view.'[24] He observes that the association of sin and sex, sex and dirt, stems 'from deep-seated psychological factors' (p. 141); he points to the 'enigmas built into our experience with sexuality' and to the frightening power of sex, which 'can wreak untold sorrow in the form of shame, jealousy, rivalry, and violence' (pp. 144, 140).

Nevertheless, Scripture does not countenance all the claims of tradition. The modern consensus that Scripture differs from heathen religions, and even from some trends in Judaism, in its refusal both to idolize sex and to blame it, appears to be well grounded. The typical ascetic figure in Israel, the Nazirite, did not abstain from marriage – an exception in the field of comparative religion. As we saw, the words of Psalm 51 do not bear the anti-sexual meaning which Augustine and tradition

---

[20] *Cf.* p. 63 for a statement equating sensuousness and sinfulness, and pp. 63ff. for the argument that the woman is more sensuous and has more anxiety than the man.

[21] *Cf.* pp. 48, 69 ('The sexual is the expression for the prodigious *Widerspruch* [contradiction] that the immortal spirit is determined as *genus*') and 71 ('spirit cannot participate in the culmination of the erotic'); the last two quotations suggest Kierkegaard's main motives.

[22] According to Gateau 1949: 10, Søren's father impressed upon the child the idea that the sexual instinct is sinful of itself (quoting the *Journals*, summer 1845).

[23] See Pannenberg 1994: 242ff. for a good account of Augustine's views.

[24] See Peters 1994: 148ff. for an example (Elaine Pagels).

attached to them. Accounting for the propagation of original sin by the disorders of human sexual life has no sufficient warrant from the Bible.

The other language of orthodox theology in dealing with original sin has been *legal* or *forensic* – Paul's language in Romans 5. Reformed theologians, especially, have erected the grand edifice of federal (covenant) theology on the foundation of its rules. It retains some metaphorical flexibility, but evangelicals will claim (and rightly so) that it is far more direct and literal than any talk of sin as infection and infirmity. Its prominence in Scripture generally, taken together with the strict consistency of its use by biblical writers, establishes this conviction. Human judges were instituted as God's representatives, wielding delegated authority from above,[25] under the transcendent reference of equity; judicial language and logic, therefore, are appropriate in describing God's relationship with humankind. The distance between *A* and *B* is minimal, and measured; metaphor slides into ontologically based analogy.

Along the 'realist' line, all are fallen and guilty because they actually fell 'in Adam' by virtue of some ontological identity: 'We were all in that one, when we were all that one.'[26] Strictly speaking, there has been no propagation, no imputation of an alien sin, for *we* were there in Eden, and *we* committed the transgression there and then. Yet realists have not been consistent. (Augustine vacillated markedly – a fact which did

---

[25] That earthly judges and rulers are raised to their position by divine appointment is presupposed and expressed everywhere in the Bible; the view that their authority is thus delegated and representative implies a further step along the same line. It surfaces in texts which use *'elōhîm* for magistrates (Ex. 21:6; 22:8f.; Ps. 82, for which I still prefer the older rabbinic, and Calvin's, interpretation) and is spelled out in Rom. 13:1ff. It is in keeping with the royal 'ideology', making the king the Lord's 'son' and 'lieutenant', and with the rich analogical play on the offices of judge and ruler, shepherd and saviour – as fulfilled by God and human beings. *Cf.* also the close association in Pr. 24:21; Ec. 8:2; 1 Pet. 2:17 (and 15?). The deeper rationale for this ordinance of God is well encapsulated in Pierre Courthial's (1972: 17) summary: 'Man is too small not to be under authority. Man is too great to be under authorities that would not be derived from God himself.'

[26] Augustine, *De Civitate Dei* XIII.14: 'Omnes enim fuimus in illo uno, quando omnes fuimus ille unus', as quoted by Williams 1927: 373 (in n. 3, he quotes Ambrose: 'Fuit Adam, et in illo fuimus omnes', 'Adam was, and in him were we all').

not escape Harnack's notice.)[27] They wish to maintain both our ontological identity with Adam and transmission of sin through the generations, and emphasize either 'seminal participation' (with the warrant of the logic of Heb. 7:10: Levi, while in his great-grandfather's loins, paid the tithe to Melchizedek) or human 'nature' considered as one entity, which was in Adam and fell in him.[28] Shedd's 'elementary invisible substance' offers a modern version of this 'realism' of the idea of humanness.[29]

The realist explanation is fraught with a number of difficulties. 'Realizing' the idea of nature so strongly that it becomes numerically one as a substance, with a history of its own, demands a rather extreme form of Platonism or (in Shedd's case) the acceptance of modern philosophical opinions which we have biblical reasons to suspect. Hebrews 7:9–10 hardly bears the weight that some would put on these verses.[30] In harmony with the writer's free method of interpreting Old Testament details, it need not signify more than the point he draws from Genesis 14, namely the subordination of the Aaronic priesthood to Melchizedek's: Levi (as a descendant) was subordinate to Abraham, Abraham was subordinate to Melchizedek (in his priesthood, at any rate), therefore the Levitical priesthood acknowledges the superior rank of Melchizedek's. Otherwise, if we were to build a theory of 'seminal participation' equivalent to identity, Hebrews 7:9–10 would prove too much: all actions of all progenitors would have to be ascribed to each of their descendants, which is nearly absurd.

What the 'realist' proposal tends to sweep under the carpet is the primary datum of individual responsibility, of individuality as such. Even if the language of extreme realism were adopted, the difficult step would still be there: how do we move from seminal participation, or ideal nature, to the distinct existence of individuals? It is *they* who stand condemned as guilty.[31] The 'vacillations' in the way Augustine and many others expressed

[27] Adolf von Harnack, *Lehrbuch der Dogmengeschichte* III, p. 215, according to Brunner 1947: 122 n. 1. On Augustine's lack of rigour, see Murray 1977: 30ff.
[28] Williams 1927: 305 n. 1 quotes Ambrose, *Apologia David altera* 71: 'Adam is in each one of us; for in him *human nature itself sinned*'; the word for 'nature', however, is *conditio*.
[29] *Cf.* above, ch. 3, n. 20.
[30] For Johnson (1974: 314f.) it is the language of typology.
[31] See the strong argument of Murray 1977: 30ff., esp. 32.

themselves witness to their sense of that difficulty; they still had to make room for plurality. Is it enough to imagine that it was there (in Eden), somehow, in compressed form? Or that 'nature' both remains singular and yet becomes plural in the multitude of individuals? The emphatic *contrast* in Romans 5 between the one man and the many lends no encouragement to a strategy that tends to minimize and dissolve individuality (so Johnson 1974: 309f.).

Lack of sensitivity to the basic fact of individual distinction and responsibility also undermines the value of broad metaphors drawn from plant or animal life. These swarm like bees when traditional theologians explain our involvement in Adam's sin. For Aquinas, 'the many human beings who are derived from Adam are as many members in one and the same body': in a body, the hand is guilty as it is moved by the will, and so the person is guilty as he or she is moved by Adam (*Summa theologiae* Ia IIae, 81.1). Calvin considers it natural that infection should spread from the root to the branches (*Institutes* II.i.6 and even more strongly 7). Hughes (1989: 132f.) follows in the footsteps of such notable predecessors when he argues that human history parallels that of a single person, who is still responsible at eighty for acts committed in his or her teens. He borrows from John Donne the illustration of the oak: 'Adam is the acorn; mankind is the tree produced from that acorn. Adam's defect is the defect of the tree of our humanity . . .' These and similar comparisons are not altogether devoid of interest, but if they purport to solve the core issue, we cannot but acknowledge their failure; they beg the question. Members in a body are not responsible individuals. Branches in a tree are not responsible individuals. Humankind is not a single person; it is many. It is at this very juncture that the whole problem lies.[32]

Along the 'federal' line, the same objections do not obtain. The doctrine preserves individual distinction. If God appointed Adam as the head of the human race, his acts rightfully counted as those of the entire community. That all members should stand under the obligation to pay the legal

---

[32] Some would still appeal to the categories of 'corporate personality', but I have shown that they are inadequate as tools for biblical reflection; they have recently received a devastating critique. See above, ch. 4, under 'Shared inheritance and individual decision', with n. 21 (pp. 93ff.).

debt agrees with legal principle and practice, biblical and otherwise.

The charge (that is often brought) that imputation is then based on a legal fiction hardly seems fair. Advocates of the federal view, such as Turretin, emphasize that the legal bond is added to the natural 'family' fellowship, the genetic commonality.[33] Furthermore, if God so appointed Adam, it is no fiction, but legal reality. Nor is it justified to require the prior consent of the individuals represented for representation to be valid.[34]

Some degree of discomfort may be felt, however, in the arguments of leading Reformed theologians, and this may betray hidden tensions in the theory. Turretin is led to state that after the fall Adam laid down his 'public person', so that he ceased to be the representative 'head' of humankind; otherwise his other acts would also be reckoned to his posterity, which they are not.[35] Jonathan Edwards struggles with the thought of Adam's function. John Murray's thorough treatment of the issue shows that Edwards does not teach 'mediate imputation' (the solution which Josué de la Place of Saumur Reformed Academy contrived and the Synod of Charenton condemned in 1645) – the theory that Adam's sin would be reckoned to his descendants on the ground of, or *mediante*, inherited depravity.[36] Edwards, however, departs from the 'federal' consensus. He is not satisfied with representation; he affirms *identity*, as a fact prior to imputation and established by divine constitution. From that it follows that Adam's sin was ours, both as the 'first arising of an evil disposition' and as the guilt of this original apostasy.[37] Edwards argues that

> . . . the objection . . . made against a supposed divine
> constitution, whereby *Adam* and his *posterity* are viewed

[33] See Turretin 1847: 557 (IX.9.11); Murray 1977: 37f.

[34] See Murray's powerful rejoinder, 1977: 36 n. 51.

[35] Turretin 1847: 566 (IX.9.36): '. . . depositam personam publicam . . . desiit tamen esse *Caput rapraesentativum* . . .'

[36] Murray 1977: 53ff., refuting such major interpreters as Charles Hodge and William Cunningham but siding with Warfield. Gerstner (1992: 328) refers to Foster, Berkhof and Boardman as being of the same opinion as Hodge.

[37] Edwards 1879: 220f. and the corresponding quotations by Murray 1977: 55ff. (he quotes from a New York, 1855, edition of the *Works*, with the indications II, 480ff.).

and treated as *one*, in the manner and for the purposes supposed – as if it were *not consistent with truth*, because no constitution can make those to be *one*, which are *not* one – is built on a false hypothesis: for it appears, that a *divine constitution* is what *makes truth* in affairs of this nature (1879: 224b).[38]

Murray (1977: 56) lucidly summarizes Edwards' idea: 'God looked on posterity as being one with Adam and looked upon their sin as coexisting with Adam's', so that 'the sin is just as directly theirs as it was his'. Edwards 'is explicating the meaning of our direct involvement in the first sin of Adam by reason of the *identity* or *oneness* of Adam and his posterity' (p. 61). Murray curiously adds, however, that this participation or derivation, for the great New England thinker, happens 'by way of imputation', an emphasis which we do not find in Edwards' text.[39] Apart from some idiosyncrasies in Murray's concept of imputation, this small discrepancy may reflect Edwards' own difficulty in maintaining both the strictest identity and yet a true diversity of individuals. For instance, he qualifies the bold proclamation that 'a divine constitution is what makes truth' by the clause 'in affairs of this nature'; and his concept of oneness is so constituted that God 'dealt with all the branches, as if they had been then existing in their root' (p. 220b). Does 'as if' imply that they were not existing truly? Gerstner takes a further step. He understands that 'according to Edwards, men do not inherit

---

[38] He stresses that continued existence of any subject *always* depends on an '*arbitrary* constitution of the Creator' (224a, *cf.* 223b).

[39] Murray (1977) constantly supplies imputation in this role. According to Murray's wording and summaries, Edwards saw 'that the sin as *imputed* must be construed as comprising the same two aspects which apply to Adam's own sin' (p. 59, but Edwards does not stress 'as imputed'); 'imputation must include the evil disposition' (p. 59); the first existing of an evil disposition, Murray says of Edwards, 'he insists is involved in the imputation of Adam's first sin' (p. 61); it 'is involved for posterity in the imputation of Adam's sin' (p. 62). Actually, according to Murray's own quotations of Edwards' words, Edwards rather underlines that the first evil disposition 'was included in' Adam's *sin*, which is directly that of his posterity (p. 57), and imputation, the charge of guilt, is only *consequent* (pp. 58, 61). We may add the clear statement: 'Therefore the sin of apostasy is not theirs, merely because God *imputes* it to them; but it is *truly* and *properly* theirs, and on that *ground* God imputes it to them' (Edwards 1879: 225b).

guilt but are punished for their own sins, for even the first sin was theirs by their own action' (1992: 329); and 'indeed it is not a doctrine of imputation – mediate or immediate' (p. 328). This, at least, goes against the letter, for Edwards does speak of imputation; the legal process does take place (and Adam himself is charged first). But Gerstner's key point is this: there is no transference in strictest identity.[40] In Gerstner's opinion, Edwards 'is not always consistent here and has a tendency to vacillate' (p. 356).[41] When giants stumble, we should look out for slippery stones in our path.

Murray himself (1977: 73ff.) is unhappy with some features of current Reformed versions of the doctrine. He takes to task Charles Hodge for his emphatic disjunction between the *reatus culpae* (the 'guilt of the fault', that is, personal blameworthiness) and the *reatus poenae* (the 'guilt of penalty', that is, legal liability).[42] With regard to Adam's sin, we inherit the latter, not the former. In response, Murray protests that 'we must not so attenuate our involvement that what is conceived of as ours is merely the judicial liability or some other consequence of sin' (p. 86). Imputation is of sin, not only of condemnation; it is as sinners that all were constituted, he underlines (p. 75).[43] His

[40] Gerstner refers to a sermon on Gn. 3:11 which denies the need for transmission of sin (p. 329); he also refers (pp. 196f.) to Peter Y. De Jong's *The Covenant Idea in New England Theology, 1620–1847* (Grand Rapids: Eerdmans, 1945) to which I had no access. In De Jong's judgment, Edwards 'removed the whole problem into the realm of metaphysics and did not a little toward weakening and finally destroying belief in original sin' (De Jong's p. 155, quoted, without Gerstner's full approval, on p. 197).

[41] Murray (1977: 53) quotes a statement of William Cunningham to the same effect.

[42] Murray demonstrates that orthodox Protestant divines criticized this conceptual pair, which Catholic theologians used. I agree that Turretin's formulation is finer and better adjusted, when he distinguishes between *reatus in actu primo, seu potentialis* (guilt in the first act, but potential) and *reatus in actu secundo seu actualis* (guilt in the second act, but actual) (1847: 538 [IX.3.2]). But I concur with J. H. Thornwell (according to Murray 1977: 80 n. 126) that the meaning or intention of Hodge's distinction is the same. It is just that Catholic theologians applied it in reverse; they claimed that people were freed from the *reatus culpae*, but not from the *reatus poenae*, at least from the obligation to bear temporal penalties (Turretin 1847: 539 [IX.3.6]).

[43] *Cf.* p. 85: 'Paul not only speaks of the wages of sin as penetrating to all, not only of the judicial condemnation as coming upon all, but also of all as implicated in the sin of Adam with the result that they become sinners.'

proposal tries to distinguish between judicial liability (not enough, in his sight) and property given in the very act, the very disobedience, of Adam (p. 88). Thus, he can claim, 'in respect of posterity, Adam's trespass was both *peccatum alienum* and *peccatum proprium*' (p. 86). Such is our oneness with Adam that 'depravity may not be conceived of so much as a penal infliction arising from the imputation of Adam's sin [the usual Reformed view] but as an implicate of solidarity with Adam in his sin' (p. 90); 'infliction with depravity is involved in the imputation of Adam's sin' (p. 92).

Murray resists, however, the temptation of identity realism. He wishes to maintain the *forensic* character of the relationship (pp. 72, 76, *etc.*). He acknowledges that the key phrase 'constituted sinners', in Romans 5:19, 'cannot be made to express any more than the forensic relation to Adam's sin' (p. 89), and he constantly speaks in terms of 'imputation'. The question arises: what is the difference, then, between Adam's sin being laid to the account of his posterity, that is, reckoned as theirs (p. 72), and their being under the obligation to satisfy justice (Hodge's words)? Murray labels the second term a 'judicial consequence' of the first, but the distance is so small (imputation being a judicial operation) that one wonders about the real import of his argument. Charging with sin means requiring payment for sin; taking guilt into account is nothing other than condemnation. The distinction over which Murray labours so hard seems either inconsequential or obscure.[44] More pertinent and of truer import is the difference (to which I have already pointed) between, on the one hand, bearing the consequences of another's sin, as members of the sinner's community may have to do (as do, for instance, children and grandchildren, and as did David's subjects stricken by the plague) – as a fact of solidarity but not imputation – and, on the other hand, sharing the obligation to satisfy justice. The issue is whether the same condemnation extends to the community or not. Inasmuch as John Murray does not reach an equivalent clarity, his efforts constitute a symptom of uneasiness within the 'federal' tradition.

---

[44] Berkouwer (1971: 461 n. 34), who has noticed the kinship with Jonathan Edwards' emphasis on our constituted oneness with Adam, comments: 'In my judgment Murray is no more successful than Edwards in making this distinction clear.'

The arguments and refinements draw attention to the main objection raised against the 'federal' solution: imputation of alien guilt strains the sense of justice in most readers. The *Formula consensus helvetici* affirms that the rightness of God's judgment in his reckoning of Adam's alien sin as his descendants' is hidden:[45] Berkouwer aptly remarks that it is this hiddenness that is the problem (1971: 457ff.). It could be maintained only on strong scriptural grounds. Yet my suggested reading of Romans 5:12–21 (see above, chapter 3) removes the only ground which was thought to be solid and secure.

Since Anselm especially, Catholic theology has focused on the negative or privative aspect of sin.[46] The fall entailed the loss of original righteousness and of the other divine gifts added in creation; since the fall, humankind is *deprived* (of them) before it is *depraved*. It is noteworthy that Calvin made room for that theme, with the only caveat that it should not become a pretext for minimizing the grievousness of sin (*Institutes* II.i.8 *et passim*). Berkouwer (1971: 479ff., esp. 481) has well perceived this feature in Calvin.[47] This may have been one factor which, for Calvin, veiled the need to account for the transmission of sin. The image of something lost looks self-evident; if Adam lost the gifts, obviously he could not pass them on.

A measure of dissatisfaction is again felt when one realizes that righteousness is not a *thing* to be added to others or withdrawn. We must avoid the trap of metaphorical language and a lazy logic based on appearances. Righteousness is disposition, behaviour, relationship. It is the absolute demand of God and the life of human life. To lack righteousness means to *practise* unrighteousness.

That all the main standard answers have their drawbacks does not entail that we should simply discard or ignore them. Rather, since none appears to be as adequate as their supporters seem to think, we should try to supplement and strengthen them. My

[45] The *Consensus*, art. X, says *judicio Dei arcano et justo*.

[46] Kenny 1975: 52; Williams 1927: 397f.; Spaemann (1991: 63) says: 'Original sin is no positive quality that each individual would inherit from his ancestors; but it is the lack of a quality that he should have inherited.' (Spaemann adds: 'the missing quality is that of belonging to a salvation community.')

[47] Pannenberg (1994: 254) states: 'The older Protestant theology, too, followed the same line, though with a special emphasis on the complementary nature of the two aspects of sin.'

strategy will first be to weaken the categorical opposition of the two elements which the doctrine combines, individual responsibility and hereditary determination (without denying the difference, and while arguing from human complexity). Secondly, I plan to draw some help from other perspectives (spiritual warfare and the 'negative' view). Finally, I shall endeavour to give more consistency to Adam's headship, and, at the same time, not to tax it as heavily as traditional doctrine does.

Second thoughts

Against too facile a use of medical metaphors, and the like, we must heed the protest that sin is a matter of willing; it belongs to the freedom exercised by individuals. But is there not a hidden assumption here that we should examine? I suspect that the terms 'biological' *versus* 'spiritual' (and so on), are treated as mutually exclusive, as radically and ultimately opposed. And this suggests a reflection of *dualism.* It should not be allowed to pass for the most elementary and obvious truth. What are we, after all, in concrete life, if not a synthesis of biology and spirit? A human being functions as an incredibly complex interaction of all levels. Pascal, again, derided the almost divine Thinker who could be stopped by a mere fly: *O ridicolisissimo eroe!*[48] The highest of our religious affections or emotions affect the chemical balance in our cells, and the reverse is also true. We are spiritual down to our toes, or to our instincts; we are living bodies right up to our mental activities, our longings, our loves. If original sin involves both, it is human indeed.

Neo-Calvinist philosophers and apologists have shown, through their search for 'ground-motives' and their transcendental critique of theoretical thought, that the modern mind has been misled and enslaved by a false antimony between nature and freedom. Both have been erected as ultimate but irreconcilable principles, each defined by the negation of the other. On the basis of divine creation and under divine sovereignty, there is a duality, to be sure; a *distinction* is certainly to be made between bodily processes and personal freedom, but no *separation.* We should not posit an absolute otherness between

---

[48] *Pensée* 95 (Lafuma), 366 (Brunschvicg). The Italian words could be rendered, 'What a most ridiculous hero – or demi-god!'

the two, but rather a harmony within God's wise ordering of his universe. As soon as the foundational reference to God is erased, each of the two terms comes to stand on its own; being absolutized, they can no longer recognize each other, but only their opposition. The idol at one end calls for the counter-idol at the other end – an insight that came also to Gustave Thibon, an independent thinker with an altogether different background: 'I discern an idol in that she is pregnant with the opposite idol' (1942: 76).[49]

The hold of the 'idolatrous' antinomy explains much of the difficulty which has been felt over original sin as being *of nature* and yet incurring *guilt*. When we break the spell, we are able to accept and even to see that will – freedom of choice – is part of human nature and brings our 'biology' into play, while this 'nature' of ours is no mere beast and does share in our privileged status as the image of God.

In view of the complexity of integration and co-operation at so many levels, the opposition of Augustinian 'generation' to Pelagian 'imitation' may be too simple. Without denying hereditary transmission in the restricted sense, it would be more helpful to stress the variety of interrelated factors. Why should we ignore the cultural heredity to which anthropologists point, when we deal with original sin? Is not moral and religious life moulded, to a great extent, by symbolic systems and language – not so much the tool of a given tongue (*cf.* Jas. 3:6) as the treasury of traditions and mores, folk wisdom and memories, works of art and literature?[50] The insights of psychology are fascinating. Think of the effect on a child's personality of damaged images of mother and father! The factors of psychic construction must be potent transmitters of the radical deformity of sin – for no mother and no father can impress the wholesome image their child needs (even a single flaw in a 'good' picture may have disastrous effects). Albert Görres (1991: 13–35) sets forth with exceptional authority and clarity the convergence between the scriptural account of sinfulness and the psychological description of our endemic cognitive and emotional disorders:

[49] The French word *idole* is of the feminine gender; hence my rendering.
[50] Paul Guilluy offers perceptive remarks in his essays in 1975a and 1975b: esp. pp. 170ff. and 176ff. in the latter.

> The various schools of Psychology, particularly Psycho-analysis, are forms of Biblical Anthropology inasmuch as they show how the human psyche has lost its integrity under the cancer-like proliferation of gnoseological, libidinous and irascible concupiscence. Psycho-analysis is the descriptive presentation of Paul's concept of the 'flesh' and John's concept of the 'world' (p. 28).

Without consenting to Jung's questionable thesis of a 'collective unconscious', the fact of unconscious influences and reactions among humankind probably hints at the reality of mysterious bonds of a psycho-spiritual nature in the community of Adam.

The insights of psychology and psycho-analysis[51] may help us to understand not only how sexuality, so central in human life, did not emerge unscathed from the tragedy of sin, but also why it is so closely bound up with the commonest apprehensions of original sin and actually contributes to its tyranny. Sexual energy untamed is such 'a wild horse', 'akin to nuclear power' (Peters 1994: 141, 144) that any weakness or flaw affecting the controlling centre of personality transforms sexuality into the threat of possible chaos.[52] And since it is intensely relational (erotic desire being ultimately the desire of the other's desire, since the desire of the one is aroused, fuelled, heightened, moulded, by the desire of the other), sexual disorder reproduces sexual disorder (and from earliest life).

The spontaneous association with *dirt* also gives pause for

---

[51] I concur with Pierre Grelot (1973: 22): 'Freud, in spite of his atheism, is consonant with the structure of biblical thought', whereas Jung is closer to Germanic (pagan) religiosity.

[52] Peters (1994: 140) sees 'the desire to maintain order in the face of possible chaos' as the root of the nearly universal moral discipline in matters of sex. Peters' realism should be emulated. His eloquent summary is worth quoting: 'Sex is explosive. When we drop our guard, it contaminates. In the context of love, it produces the greatest experience of tenderness. Apart from love, it can be abusive and dehumanizing. In short, sex is a supra-individual power of considerable force, an ambiguous force that sometimes lends us energy and at other times seeks to control us from within. The task of ethics with regard to our sexuality, it would seem, is to provide guidance and control that will ensure that it is wholesomely productive and not wantonly destructive' (p. 144).

reflection (pp. 141f.).[53] It has links with our reaction to bodily fluids generally – probably a defence of individual integrity – and to an obvious anatomical conjunction;[54] but deeper unconscious factors probably come into play.[55] Some emphases of feminist theologies, which major on male violence,[56] could be added to this analysis: part of the historic misogyny of societies and of the church stems from a deep-seated fear of sex and a resentment of the inability to master it; the woman both fascinates and frightens, not because of what she inherently is, but as the perceived embodiment of the untameable power of sexuality.[57] In older usage in both French and English, 'the sex' meant 'the female sex'. Such is the interaction of influences that shape the human mind and soul that the poor condition of our sexuality offers a handy vehicle for the spread of sinfulness.

Dare I mention genetics? Even genetics should not be ruled out of court, since the discipline deals with one level in the complex interaction of elements. We should exclude the fantasy about a 'sin gene' or sin as a chromosomic aberration; this is far too crude, and a category error. But could there be a far more subtle disorder of the genetic formula and of its expression, a disorder which would correlate to spiritual deformation? Might we imagine, for instance, that spiritual integrity could support protective or restorative mechanisms against detrimental mutations – mechanisms which were lost? Peters (pp. 304ff.) makes

---

[53] Peters refers here to Ricœur and to L. William Countryman, *Dirt, Greed, and Sex* (Philadelphia: Fortress, 1988).

[54] Augustine noted once that we are born *inter faeces et urinam* – an incontrovertible fact, which leaves open the question (impossible to answer) of God's design for the ways of human reproduction apart from the fall.

[55] Those factors are probably involved in the relationship to the mother, and in the need to gain separation from her.

[56] See Suchocki 1994: esp. 129: 'A bent toward violence built into the human species, the solidarity of the race wherein each is affected by the deeds of all others and affects the future of all others, and finally the unique structures of intersubjectivity that mediate the values of one generation to the next, all conspire to create conditions for each human individual that are analogous to the ancient concept of original sin. To be human is to be embroiled in sin before one even has the means to assent.' For most feminists, violence is primarily, if not exclusively, male.

[57] Peters (1994: 151ff.) sketches a penetrating analysis (see p. 153 for the influence of the monastic ideal and discipline).

bold to recommend dialogue between geneticists and theologians. He observes the 'curious situation' in which contemporary theologians affirming original sin are most reluctant to think of biological transmissibility, whereas natural scientists are hotly debating whether behaviour traditionally defined as sinful can be genetically inherited (p. 327).

François Turretin, within the limits of the resources available to him, made a beginning in the direction I have been suggesting. He tried to maintain some kind of bodily transmission of original sin *without* any physical contact or any action of the body upon the soul,

> . . . but through *the most narrow conjunction of soul and body in one hypostasis* [person] and their intimate *sympathy* for each other, and mutual appetite and inclination, so that they most tightly embrace and affect each other, and so that, just as the body tends toward the soul as toward its perfection and good, thus the soul should tend toward the body as toward its proper abode and the instrument of its actions (1847: 581 [IX.12.16], my translation).

Whereas, he argues, sin is not found in the body formally and fully realized, it can be found 'inchoatively, dispositionally and radically in the body as the proper abode of the soul, soon to be united to the soul into one *hypostasis*'; 'through the vital and animal spirits of the foetus' sin may be imprinted upon the soul, just as children do not receive from their parents actual diseases such as gout and callouses, but 'certain impressions which are the principles of these diseases' (p. 579 [IX.12.8]). Obviously, Turretin is looking for a solution in the complexity of human life.

In a word, this human complexity could bear the biblical name 'flesh', and the above comments could be summarized in the proposition 'What is born of the flesh is flesh' (Jn. 3:6).

The sway of evil powers over human life could further enrich and complicate the picture. I did not mention this earlier, since it is not found in the Romans 5 'seat of doctrine', and the classic disputes of our tradition have left it out. But Ephesians 2 does conjoin the 'prince of aerial authority' with wrath-deserving 'nature'. In the story of Eden, in Genesis 3, the fall did mean 'leaving it to the snake'[58] – yielding to the occult power 'who is called Devil and Satan, who seduces the whole inhabited earth' (Rev. 12:9). I shall not enter here into the wide and disputed field of demonology and 'spiritual warfare',[59] but shall *cautiously* refer to some pastoral evidence of encroachment by evil spirits on human lineage; if confirmed, it would strengthen the case of heredity in sinfulness. The fact that 'the whole world lies in [the power of] the Evil One' (1 Jn. 5:19) has something to do, we may presume, with the propagation of original sin.

The contrast between a 'positive' and a 'negative' understanding of sin should not be pressed. Both may assist us in the right assessment of the data. The 'negative' or 'privative' view does not amount to mere attenuation of the good. Privation can be atrocious and devastating; Turretin offers helpful nuances on this point.[60] The metaphor of loss agrees with the kinship of evil and nothingness in Scripture. The theme of 'added' gifts in the beginning is not devoid of biblical support; Eden is 'added' to the earth, and such an addition demonstrates how covenant partners have an *interest* in history. If this is so, we should not despise the facility of negative language. Apparently, the metaphor of gifts lost has helped major thinkers (Calvin) to understand how Adam's disobedience dramatically affected his posterity.

The mere deprivation of God's fellowship in foetal life, I suggest, would already be enough severely to disturb the construction of personality. Jonathan Edwards (1879: 219a) strongly insisted on the effect of the mere removal of original graces:

> Only God's *withdrawing*, as it was highly proper and necessary that he should, from rebel man, and his [man's] *natural* principles being *left to themselves*, is

[58] See above, ch. 4, n. 14.

[59] From the flood of recently published material on the issue, I would recommend the symposium edited by Wagner and Pennoyer (1990) and the erudite study by Arnold (1992).

[60] For Turretin (1847: 575 [IX.1.1, *cf*. para. 7]), it is not sufficient to speak of a mere lack of righteousness. On p. 577 (para. 16) he accepts the idea of privation 'active and efficacious' (*actuosa et efficax*), involving a depraved disposition. This is standard Reformed doctrine (*cf.* Berkouwer 1971: 63f.).

sufficient to account for his becoming entirely corrupt,
and bent on sinning against God.

Kierkegaard's understanding of anxiety/dread as the 'vertigo'
of freedom presupposes a spiritual vacuum around freedom –
that is, a fallen, alienated, condition. In the beginning, it was not
so, when the creature of divine delight was bathed continually in
the sunshine of God's favour. But anxiety, which brings forth
sinful attitudes, was inevitable as soon as humankind lost its
spiritual environment of love.

Clarification of what is meant by 'transmission' may also clear
the way of unnecessary stumbling-blocks. With all due respect to
the Reformed theology to which I am indebted, I have been led
to question the doctrine of alien guilt transferred – that is, the
doctrine of the imputation to all of Adam's own trespass, his act
of transgression. If Scripture definitely taught such a doctrine,
however offensive to modern taste, I should readily bow to its
authority. But where does Scripture require it? My investigation
did not find it in the only passage from which it is drawn,
Romans 5. Could it be, then, a case of laying heavy burdens
upon people's shoulders, beyond the express demands of God?

The following scheme seems to suit the language and logic of
the Bible. Alienation from God, the condition of being deprived
and depraved, follows immediately upon the first act of sinning
– for Adam himself and for his seed after him. It affects his
descendants from the very start of their existence, because of
their relationship to him. It is voluntary inasmuch as it implies a
disposition of the will, even in its most embryonic form; it is
guilty.

Is it a 'state'? The contrast between act and state is somewhat
blurred;[61] just as every human act has duration, temporal
extension, so a spiritual state, a state of the will, is activity
constantly renewed, moment by moment. The old concept of
habitus, a disposition, a 'having' (which is a verbal form!) may
still be the most convenient one here. We underline the fact that
original sin so conceived is not only 'potential' but *actual*, from

---

[61] Against Brunner's statements: 'Sin is never a state, but it is always act' (1947:
148); 'Sin, even of Original Sin, is always *actus* . . .', but he concedes
immediately, 'even if it is not a momentary act which can be isolated' (p. 117
n. 2). Also Kierkegaard 1980: 15, 21.

the start, as is foetal and infant life itself. The will, though undeveloped, does exist, and its anti-God tendency already constitutes a wilful exercise.

Being born sinners is not a penalty, or strictly the result of transference, but simply an existential, spiritual, *fact* for human beings since Adam. It may be significant that Johnson (1974: 315) should fall back on the language of spiritual fact after confessing the difficulty of the 'alien sin' concept: 'Adam's posterity cannot claim to have ever been innocent. They enter existence depraved and guilty, having the same legal status and moral nature as their head *ab initio*.'

Now, if this simpler perspective rids us of dubious reasoning about guilt transference, it does not put an end to all questioning. The theological mind is not satisfied with brute fact. Can we see how it is *right*, under the righteous God's sovereign rule, that Adam's descendants find themselves deprived of the gift of divine fellowship, and therefore enmeshed in a destructive disorder at all levels of their nature, which affects heredity; and that they find themselves the slaves of their own pride, greed, lies and fears, under the tyranny of the Evil One?

I propose that the decisive consideration, when we search for the rightness of the 'fact', remains the headship, or capitate, structure – the organic solidarity of the race, the spiritual dimension of humanity's oneness. The 'fact' basically represents the outworking of the structure, once the head has made the wrong choice. The analogy of nationhood may be the least inadequate: when a head of state declares war on another nation, all children born during the war are at war with the other nation. In Adam's case, the consequence operates at a much deeper level, because our Adamic (that is, human) solidarity is more essential, and because the relationship is to God 'in whom we live and move and have our being'. Thus the spiritual war involves an actual enmity in the will of every member of the community. Enmity towards God carries guilt.

We may point to the meaning of human procreation. The mandate and blessing of Genesis 1:28 is that the male and female should multiply; we call it 'reproduction'. With the warrant of Genesis 5:3, fathers beget children as their own images and likenesses. Since procreation is not merely biological, but is also human, it is no wonder that the determinant of the father's condition should be reproduced in the son's. Fallen Adam multiplies as fallen, and 'what is born of the flesh is flesh'. It is a fact that generates tragic consequences, but a rightful fact nevertheless.

Adam's headship, moreover, involves a deeper privilege than ordinary fatherhood. It includes the dignity of defining what it means to be human. Being human is equivalent to bearing his image (1 Cor. 15:49) – this is how we come to be, and to be what we are. We are created 'in Adam'. Hence the impossibility of the blessing of divine fellowship remaining on Adam's descendants after he had rebelled.

If individuals wish to protest, on what ground may they do so? I can see no ground for them to stand upon, no fulcrum for their plea, since their individual freedom has no independent, self-existent consistency. God created it as he created them, in and through Adam, as part of their Adamic nature. To refuse the logic of our human dependence would mean suppressing oneself, including one's sense of equity and one's ability to protest. Let protesters prove their independent freedom by dissociating themselves from Adamic sin in the way they actually behave; let them free themselves from that universal bondage portrayed by the apostle Paul: 'No, there is none, not even one' (Rom. 3:10, quoting Ps. 14:3).

Has the riddle become less opaque? My thesis offers no magic formula. It makes no claim to master mystery, or to dissect Adam's causality, or to understand the mechanisms of our solidarity with him. My proposal differs from the current 'federal' solution in three ways. First, I see no necessity for the idea that alien guilt was transferred (that is, that Adam's particular act was reckoned to the account of all). This idea is repugnant to common moral taste (including that of Christians), and finds no support in Scripture. Secondly, my proposal emphasizes loss or deprivation in a relational framework (which immediately entails guilty depravity), since the rightness of the consequence 'from Adam to his seed' is more easily perceived from that angle. Thirdly, Adam's legal capacity as the representative of the race is buttressed by a wider conception of his headship. I am conscious of meeting Jonathan Edwards' concerns at some points, but I avoid positing such a strict identity (between Adam and his descendants) that individual distinction seems to be lost, and that the divine constitution is made to look arbitrary because the emphasis falls on Adam's singular deed.

My stress on 'fact', on the legitimate outworking of a basic creation structure of humankind, will not silence all indignation. An inborn state, or *habitus*, of guilt without any prior deliberation at a 'neutral' stage will be denounced by some as intolerably unjust. The root of this reaction, however, is clearly the absolutization of individual freedom. It must be dealt with at a deeper level of theological and philosophical reflection.

Freedom, the protest will go, is not a thing to be derived from another, or multiplied, or twisted and truncated. This protest amounts to a denial of the headship structure, the mystery of which is ultimately the mystery of *created freedom*. How can freedom be created? This is the very mystery of creation – I do not claim to master it. Nevertheless, the coherence of scriptural teaching, and the way it illuminates human experience, lead me to feel that my thesis is not vulnerable to pressures it cannot bear. Such considerations as I have adduced facilitate an appreciation of the well-measured realism of the doctrine of original sin without undue anxiety or timidity.

This can also be seen, paradoxically, as a preamble to good news.

A gate of hope

What might seem to be a gloomy speculation, a 'Valley of Achor', can in fact be renamed a 'gate of hope' (Ho. 2:15).

We have already seen that denials of original sin may lead to harsher judgments and to deeper despair than does the Augustinian doctrine.[62] The church dogma is more merciful than some 'optimistic' assessments of human reality. Since it reveals all individuals to be victims of bondage as well as evil by their own responsibility, it invites, indeed induces, compassion. This benefit did not escape Jonathan Edwards' (1897: 230a) sensitive appraisal:

> This doctrine teaches us to think no worse of others, than of ourselves: it teaches us that we are *all*, as we are by nature, *companions* in a miserable helpless con-

[62] This is a leitmotiv of Gesché 1993.

dition; which under a revelation of the divine mercy, tends to promote mutual *compassion*.

Scripture itself shows us the Lord moved to fatherly pity when he sees the souls he has made failing and fainting (Is. 57:16).

But there is more. Romans 5, as we have read it, unfolds a parallel that is more than a parallel. The apostle sets forth an *a fortiori* argument which makes Adam's role in the spread of sin the *presupposition* of Christ's redeeming work, and thus only can he proclaim its powerful reversal (vv. 15ff.).

The relationship appears to be twofold. In order to defeat the dominion of evil, Scripture tells us, the Redeemer had to come in Adamic flesh, in the very likeness of sinful flesh, to break the power of sinfulness in the flesh (Rom. 8:3). He had to enter humanity, to become a son of Adam (*cf.* Lk. 3:38), and to share in the communal life of the race, in order to be able to take upon himself 'the sin of the world'. The spiritual solidarity of humankind was, it seems, a prerequisite of his sin-bearing office, regarding both the 'synthesis' of all sins as the sin (singular!) of the world, and the possibility of transference. He did not intervene to help angels, whose nature, presumably, is purely individual (Heb. 2:16).

Had he been 'in Adam', however, under that first head, he would have been born a sinner as all other children of Adam are, in a state of enmity towards God. He would have been unfit for any atoning substitution. But because of his personal pre-existence, he did not depend totally on Adam, he did not owe his individual existence to Adam, and so he was not in Adam. He did not fall under Adam's headship. His birth could mark a new beginning in the life of humankind. He could become a new head, a second and final Adam (1 Cor. 15:45ff.). Knowing no sin and yet truly joined to Adam's posterity, he could freely take upon himself the communal guilt of his fellow humans.

Jesus Christ accomplished the work of redemption as the new Adam, as the head for the body, as the pioneer (*archēgos*), the path-opener (Latin *dux*, 'leader') whom the others follow and who, as their leader, can freely take responsibility for those who belong to him. This was brought to light on 'the first day of the week', that is, the eighth day of creation, the day the new creation dawned. He rose again as the pioneer of life, the firstfruits of his own conquest over sin and death, the Adam of the new creation. He thus secured, for their benefit, ultimate dominion over the living (Rom. 14:9). The same headship structure which was effective in Adam's case still operates, but for salvation, and this is why we enjoy the fruit of his death and resurrection only when we are members of his body.

The way the new structure, or the new outworking of the structure, is grafted upon the old deserves our full notice. The new creation of which Jesus Christ is the risen head is no foreign, separate work. Its object is the first creation. Based on Christ's atoning obedience, it means the re-creation of the old, a salvation for the children of Adam. This is why Christ is the 'brother', not the 'father' as Adam was.[63] This is also why the operation of the new creation, which requires a transcendent agency, differs from the Adamic way. The spread of right-eousness and life does not follow the course of nature. It is not of the flesh but of the Spirit (Jn. 3:6). It requires a 'new birth', brought about by the Spirit and the Word.[64]

Yet since the object of redeeming grace is the same human creature, the multi-levelled complexity of our 'functioning' is also put to work in the transmission of the last Adam's righteousness and life. For this transmission involves a new community, a new symbolic system, a new kind of language which is taught and learnt and passed on from generation to generation. The role of the church may be seen in that light.

Since the fruit of Christ's work is applied to our Adamic humanity, this operation takes place in the old world of corrupted nature, and so it takes time; it is a process with several stages. We still live 'in the flesh' (Gal. 2:20). In spite of the reality of the new creation within us, as the firstfruits of the final harvest (Rom. 8:23), as the down-payment of the promised inheritance (2 Cor. 1:22; 5:5; Eph. 1:14), our children are born

[63] Although, in some respects, Christ's brotherhood resembles a fatherhood; hence his occasional use of 'children' as a form of address and, especially, Heb. 2:13f.

[64] In the light of the somewhat complex relationship of Christ's headship to that of Adam, I would deal with the controversial issue of the extent of substitution in the following way. (1) Christ definitely acted and suffered as the head of his body, as the Adam of the new humankind, that is, for those who were going to become his members through believing in him (the elect). (2) Yet he took in charge the *race*, and the sin of the race as organically one (the sin of the *world*), so that unbelievers are better viewed as branches cut off from the redeemed whole. *Cf.* Blocher 1991: esp. 99–102.

'in Adam' still; 'by nature [they are] children of wrath, as the rest of people' (Eph. 2:3). It is noteworthy that Calvin sharply rebuked those who would teach otherwise.[65]

Since we still live in the flesh, we (Christians) may not imagine that we are unaffected by substantial remnants of original sin. Whatever one's preferred interpretation of Romans 7, the present conflict between the flesh and the Spirit (Gal. 5:16ff.)[66] illustrates that our inborn disorder and the guilty disorientation of the human will still bears on Christian life. In this transition period of salvation history (where we are pilgrims on the way, in the process of being saved, and have not yet reached the goal) enough is left of original sin not only to serve as fuel (*fomes*) for sin, as traditional Catholicism had it, but to be denounced as sin and the source of guilt. As Turretin (1847: 578 [IX.11.23]) stresses, the fact that there is no longer any *condemnation* does not mean that there is nothing *condemnable*. He offers a fine summary:

> Though, indeed, we affirm that regeneration removes the *guilt and stain of original sin* as concerns *dominion*, since it is no more reckoned unto damnation and no longer reigns in the regenerate, we deny that it removes them absolutely, as concerns *existence*, and that it removes what in it has the nature and status [*rationem*] of sin (p. 577 [IX.11.21]).

When we confess this residual sinfulness, the Spirit daily applies to us the benefits of the work of our Head, to cleanse us again and again and concretely to free us from the bondage of corruption (1 Jn. 1:6 – 2:2; Rom. 8:1–14, and many other passages).

Experiencing the doctrine builds faith, and gives us solid ground for a sober, patient hope. The way to avail oneself of the victory which broke the power of original sin and all indwelling sin is to 'obey the structure', to cling to the Head (Col. 2:19), from within the living complexity of the Body.

[65] *Institutes* II.i.7; *cf.* III.xxiv.10 (against the idea that some might harbour an innate seed of election).

[66] This remains true even if one adopts Sylvain Romérowski's (1995) rather convincing argument that the 'flesh' in this passage is equivalent to the 'old man'.

If individuals wish to protest against the Adamic determination of our existence, there is a way of escaping the wilful necessity of sinful flesh, the tyranny of the kingdom of death: moving from the first allegiance and headship to the new allegiance and headship. One must first move (repentance),[67] and then cling to the Head.

The vision in Revelation 10:9–10 employs a strange symbolism, a refinement of Ezekiel's (3:3). The divine message is bitter to the belly, while it tastes like honey in the prophet's mouth. The belly (the bowels) represents the emotional level, whereas honey signals the absolute goodness of the Word of God as such. In its teaching on original sin, Scripture seems to impose a bitter diet, which causes pain at the level of our emotions: but how sweet it is, in the sense of *goodness*, for those who can taste it – the life-giving truth of Christ!

---

[67] Warfield's analysis (1970b: 280f.) is worth mentioning; Christian repentance is 'fundamentally' of original sin in the broader sense, as the sinful state in which human beings are found; but there can be no repentance of Adam's act of sinning, only a sensitive identification which 'quicken[s] within us something which very closely simulates repentance'.

Bibliography

Alexander, Joseph Addison (1953 reissue, two vols. in one), *Commentary on the Prophecies of Isaiah*. Grand Rapids: Zondervan.

Arnold, Clinton E. (1992), *Ephesians: Power and Magic. The Concept of Power in Ephesians in Light of Its Historical Setting*. 2nd edn. Grand Rapids: Baker (1st edn 1989 in *SNTS* monograph series).

Barth, Karl (1956), *Church Dogmatics* IV/1, trans. G. W. Bromiley. Edinburgh: T. and T. Clark (German original 1953).

——(1957), *Church Dogmatics* II/2, trans. G. W. Bromiley. Edinburgh: T. and T. Clark (German original 1942).

Berdiaev (Berdyaev), Nicolas (1975), *Christianisme Marxisme. Conception chrétienne et conception marxiste de l'histoire*, trans. and introduced by Laurent Gagnebin, Paris: le Centurion.

Berkouwer, G. C. (1971), *Sin*, trans. Philip C. Holtrop. Grand Rapids: Eerdmans (Dutch original in two vols., 1959 and 1960).

Bible annotée, les Prophètes, vol. 1, par une société de théologiens et de pasteurs [mainly Frédéric Godet]. Paris–Neuchâtel–Genève: Sandoz, Fischbacher, Desrogis, n.d.

Bible du rabbinat (1899), Zadoc Kahn (ed.). Paris: Durlacher.

Blocher, Henri (1984), *In the Beginning. The Opening Chapters of Genesis*, trans. David G. Preston. Leicester and Downers Grove, Ill.: IVP (French original 1979, 1st edn).

——(1989) 'Biblical Narrative and Historical Reference', in Nigel M. de S. Cameron (ed.), *Issues in Faith and History*, 102–122. Edinburgh: Rutherford House Books.

——(1991), 'The Scope of Redemption and Modern Theology', *Scottish Bulletin of Evangelical Theology* 9, 80–103.

——(1994), *Evil and the Cross*, trans. David G. Preston. Leicester: Apollos, and Downers Grove, Ill.: IVP (French original 1990).

Bruce, F. F. (1984), *The Epistles to the Colossians, to Philemon, and to the Ephesians*. New International Commentary on the New Testament. Grand Rapids: Eerdmans.

Brunner, Emil (1947), *Man in Revolt. A Christian Anthropology*, trans. Olive Wyon. Philadelphia: Westminster Press (German original 1937).

——(1952), *The Christian Doctrine of Creation and Redemption. Dogmatics*, vol. 2, trans. Olive Wyon. London: Lutterworth (German original 1950).

Bultmann, Rudolf (1952), *Theology of the New Testament*, vol. 1, trans. Kendrick Grobel. London: SCM (German original 1948).

Burton, Edward de W. (1894), *Syntax of the Moods and Tenses in New Testament Greek*. 2nd edn. Edinburgh: T. and T. Clark.

Calvez, Jean-Yves (1970), *La Pensée de Karl Marx*. New revised edn. Paris: le Seuil (1st edn 1956).

Calvin, John (1957 edn), *Institutes of the Christian Religion*, trans. Henry Beveridge. London: James Clarke.

Cassuto, Umberto (1961), *A Commentary on the Book of Genesis, Part I: From Adam to Noah, Genesis I–VI 8*, trans. Israel Abrahams. Jerusalem: Magnes, Hebrew University.

Cioran, Emmanuel (1987), *Histoire et utopie*. Folio-Essais. Paris: Gallimard.

Clemens, David M. (1994), 'The Law of Sin and Death: Ecclesiastes and Genesis 1 – 3'. *Themelios* 19/3: 5–8.

Courthial, Pierre (1972), 'Parole de Dieu et pouvoirs', *Ichthus* 22: 12–24; 23: 33–36.

Cox, Harvey (1964), *On Not Leaving It to the Snake*. New York: Macmillan.

Cranfield, C. E. B. (1975). *A Critical and Exegetical Commentary on the Epistle to the Romans*. International Critical Commentary. 2 vols. Edinburgh: T. and T. Clark.

Davis, John Jefferson (1980), 'Genesis, Inerrancy and the Antiquity of Man', in Roger R. Nicole and J. Ramsay Michaels (eds.), *Inerrancy and Common Sense*, 137–159. Grand Rapids: Baker Book House.

De Vries, Simon J. (1962), 'Sin, Sinners', in *Interpreter's Dictionary of the Bible* 4. Nashville: Abingdon Press, 361a–376a.

Delhaye, Philippe (1975), Préface, in Paul Guilluy (ed.), *La Culpabilité fondamentale. Péché originel et anthropologie moderne*, iii–vii. Gembloux: J. Duculot. Lille: Centre interdisciplinaire des Facultés catholiques.

Denton, Michael (1985), *Evolution. A Theory in Crisis*. London: Burnett.

Derousseaux, Louis (1975), 'L'Ancien Testament', in Paul

Guilluy (ed.), *La Culpabilité fondamentale. Péché originel et anthropologie moderne*, 5–25. Gembloux: J. Duculot. Lille: Centre interdisciplinaire des Facultés catholiques.

Dickson, William P. (1883), *St Paul's Use of the Terms Flesh and Spirit*. Glasgow: James MacLehose and Sons.

Dubarle, A. M. (1967), *Le Péché originel dans l'Ecriture*. Lectio divina 20. 2nd revised edn. Paris: Cerf. (1st edn 1958).

Dunn, James D. G. (1988), *Romans 1–8*. Word Biblical Commentary 38A. Dallas: Word Books.

Dupont-Sommer, André (1987), 'Ecrits qoumrariens, V: Hymnes', in André Dupont-Sommer and Marc Philonenko (eds.), *La Bible. Ecrits intertestamentaires*. Paris: NRF-Gallimard.

Edwards, Jonathan (1879), *The Great Doctrine of Original Sin Defended: Evidence of its Truth Produced and Arguments to the Contrary Answered* . . . The Works of Jonathan Edwards 1, 143–233. London: William Tegg (first edn 1758).

Evans, Craig A. (1992), 'Typology', in Joel B. Green, Scot McKnight and I. Howard Marshall (eds.), *Dictionary of Jesus and the Gospels*, 862a–866b. Leicester and Downers Grove, Ill.: IVP.

Fitzmyer, Joseph A. (1993), 'The Consecutive Meaning of EPH' HO in Romans 5.12'. *New Testament Studies* 39, 321–339.

Freud, Sigmund (1960), *A General Introduction to Psychoanalysis*, trans. Joan Riviere. New York: Washington Square Press (German original 1916–17).

Frost, Francis (1975a), 'Le Concile de Trente et la doctrine protestante', in Paul Guilluy (ed.), *La Culpabilité fondamentale. Péché originel et anthropologie moderne*, 80–105. Gembloux: J. Duculot. Lille: Centre interdisciplinaire des Facultés catholiques.

——(1975b), 'Le Concile de Trente et le péché originel: les canons et leur élaboration', in Paul Guilluy (ed.), *La Culpabilité fondamentale. Péché originel et anthropologie moderne*, 69–79. Gembloux: J. Duculot. Lille: Centre interdisciplinaire des Facultés catholiques.

Gagey, Jacques (1982), *Freud et le christianisme. Existence chrétienne et Pratique de l'inconscient*. Paris: Desclée.

Garlington, Don B. (1994), *Faith, Obedience, and Perseverance. Aspects of Paul's Letter to the Romans*. Wissenschaftliche Untersuchungen zum Neuen Testament 79. Tübingen: J. C. B. Mohr [Paul Siebeck].

Gateau, Jean-J. (1949), Introduction to his translation (made with Knud Ferlov) of Kierkegaard's *Traité du désespoir*. Paris: Gallimard.

Gauchet, Marcel (1993), Interview, in *le Nouvel Observateur* 1508, 18.

Geach, Peter T. (1977), *Providence and Evil*. Cambridge: Cambridge University Press.

Gerstner, John H. (1992), *The Rational Biblical Theology of Jonathan Edwards* 2. Powhatan, Va.: Berea Publications. Orlando, Fl.: Ligonier Ministries.

Gesché, Adolphe (1993), *Dieu pour penser* I: *le mal*. Paris: Cerf.

Gibert, Pierre (1986), *Bible, mythes et récits de commencement*. Paris: Seuil.

Girard, René (1978), *Des choses cachées depuis la fondation du monde. Recherches avec Jean-Michel Oughourlian et Guy Lefort*. Paris: Bernard Grasset.

Goldsworthy, Graeme (1987), *Gospel and Wisdom. Israel's Wisdom Literature in the Christian Life*. Biblical Classics Library. Carlisle: Paternoster.

Gordis, Robert (1957), 'The Knowledge of Good and Evil in the Old Testament and in the Qumran Scrolls', *Journal of Biblical Literature* 76, 123–138.

Görres, Albert (1991), 'Psychologische Bemerkungen über die Erbsünde und ihre Folgen', in Ch. Schönborn *et al.*, *Zur kirchlichen Erbsündenlehre. Stellungnahmen zu einer brennenden Frage*, 13–35. Einsiedeln, Freiburg: Johannes Verlag.

Grelot, Pierre (1973), *Péché originel et rédemption examinés à partir de l'épître aux Romains. Essai théologique*. Paris: Desclée.

Gross, Julius (1960–72), *Enstehungsgeschichte des Erbsündedogmas*, 4 vols. Munich: E. Reinhardt.

Guilluy, Paul (1975a), 'Sciences humaines et péché de l'humanité', in Paul Guilluy (ed.), *La Culpabilité fondamentale. Péché originel et anthropologie moderne*, 165–174. Gembloux: J. Duculot. Lille: Centre interdisciplinaire des Facultés catholiques.

——(1975b), 'Sens moderne de la culpabilité fondamentale', in Paul Guilluy (ed.), *Culpabilité fondamentale. Péché originel et anthropologie moderne*, 175–191. Gembloux: J. Duculot. Lille: Centre interdisciplinaire des Facultés catholiques.

Gundry, Robert H. (1993), *Mark. A Commentary on his Apology for the Cross*. Grand Rapids: Eerdmans.

Gundry, Robert H. (1980), 'The Moral Frustration of Paul Before his Conversion: Sexual Lust in Romans 7:7–25', in Donald A. Hagner and Murray J. Harris (eds.), *Pauline Studies. Essays Presented to Professor F. F. Bruce on his 70th Birthday*, 228–245. Exeter: Paternoster. Grand Rapids: Eerdmans.

Heddebaut, Claude (1975), 'Biologie et péché originel', in Paul Guilluy (ed.), *Culpabilité fondamentale. Péché originel et anthropologie moderne*, 153–164. Gembloux: J. Duculot. Lille: Centre interdisciplinaire des Facultés catholiques.

Hensel, Robert (1975), 'Fruit: *Karpos*', in Colin Brown (ed.), *The New International Dictionary of New Testament Theology* 1, 721–723. Grand Rapids: Zondervan.

Hess, Richard S. (1990), 'Splitting the Adam: The Usage of *'ādām* in Genesis i–v', in J. A. Emerton (ed.), *Studies in the Pentateuch*. Supplements to *Vetus Testamentum* 41, 1–15. Leiden: E. J. Brill.

Hodge, Charles (1838), *A Commentary on the Epistle to the Romans*. 2nd edn. London: Religious Tract Society.

Hoonacker, Albin van (1918), 'Is the Narrative of the Fall a Myth?' [W. Robertson Nicoll's] *The Expositor*, 8th series, 16, 373–400.

Hooker, M. D. (1959–60), 'Adam in Romans 1', *New Testament Studies* 6.

Hughes, Philip Edgcumbe (1989), *The True Image. The Origin and Destiny of Man in Christ*. Grand Rapids: Eerdmans. Leicester: IVP.

Johnson, Philip E. (1991), *Darwin on Trial*. Washington, DC: Regnery Gateway.

Johnson, S. Lewis, Jr (1974), 'Romans 5:12 – An Exercise in Exegesis and Theology', in Richard N. Longenecker and Merrill C. Tenney (eds.), *New Dimensions in New Testament Study*, 298–316. Grand Rapids: Zondervan.

Jüngel, Eberhard (1977), *Gott als Geheimnis der Welt*. Tübingen: J. C. B. Mohr [Paul Siebeck].

Kant, Immanuel (1960), *Religion Within the Limits of Reason Alone*, trans. Theodore M. Greene and Hoyt H. Hudson. Harper Torchbooks. New York: *etc.*: Harper and Row (German original 1793).

Kenny, J. P. (1975), 'The Doctrine of Original Sin from Augustine to the Present Day', in John J. Scullion *et al.*, *Original Sin*, 48–63. Victoria, Australia: Dove Communications.

Kierkegaard, Søren (1980), *The Concept of Anxiety. A Simple Psychologically Orienting Deliberation on the Dogmatic Issue of Hereditary Sin*, trans. Reidar Thomte in collaboration with Albert B. Anderson. Princeton: Princeton University Press (Danish original 1844).

Kirwan, Christopher (1988), *Augustine. The Arguments of Philosophers*. London: Routledge.

Kristeva, Julia (1980), *Pouvoirs de l'horreur. Essai sur l'abjection*. Paris: Seuil.

Kuiper, Herman (1928), *Calvin on Common Grace*. Goes, Netherlands: Oosterbaan and Le Cointre.

Lejeune, Jérôme (1968), 'Adam et Eve ou le monogenisme', *Nouvelle Revue Théologique* 90.

Lewis, C. S. (1940), *The Problem of Pain*. London: Geoffrey Bles.

Liébaert, Jacques (1975), 'La Tradition patristique jusqu'au Ve siècle', in Paul Guilluy (ed.), *La Culpabilité fondamentale. Péché originel et anthropologie moderne*. Gembloux: J. Duculot. Lille: Centre interdisciplinaire des Facultés catholiques.

Ligier, Louis (1960), *Péché d'Adam et péché du monde. Bible, Kippur, Eucharistie* 1: *l'Ancien Testament*. Coll. Théologie. Paris: Aubier.

——(1961), *Péché d'Adam et péché du monde. Bible, Kippur, Eucharistie* 2: *le Nouveau Testament*. Coll. Théologie. Paris: Aubier.

Lohse, Eduard (1986), *Die Texte aus Qumran Hebräisch und Deutsch*. 4th edn. Munich: Kösel Verlag.

Lubac, Henri de (1947), *Catholicisme. Les aspects sociaux du dogme*. 4th revised edn. Paris: le Cerf (1st edn 1938).

Lucas, Ernest C. (1987), 'Some Scientific Issues Related to the Understanding of Genesis 1 – 3', *Themelios* 12/2, 46–51.

Lyonnet, Stanislas (1963), 'Péché: IV. Dans le Nouveau Testament', in *Supplément au Dictionnaire de la Bible* 7, fasc. 38, 486–567. Paris: Letouzey et Ané.

Maillot, Alphonse, and André Lelièvre (1966), *Les Psaumes* 2. Geneva: Labor et Fides.

Malina, B. J. (1969), 'Some Observations on the Origin of Sin in Judaism and St Paul', *Catholic Biblical Quarterly* 31, 18–34.

Mannoni, O. (1968), *Freud*. Paris: Seuil.

Margot, Jean-Claude (1979), *Traduire sans trahir*. Lausanne: l'Age d'homme.

Martelet, Gustave (1986), *Libre Réponse à un scandale. La faute originelle, la souffrance, la mort*. Paris: Cerf.

Moo, Douglas J. (1991), *Romans 1 – 8*. Wycliffe Exegetical Commentary. Chicago: Moody.

Morris, Leon (1988), *The Epistle to the Romans*. Leicester: IVP. Grand Rapids: Eerdmans.

Motyer, J. A. (1993), *The Prophecy of Isaiah*. Leicester: IVP.

Murray, John (1962), 'Sin', in J. D. Douglas *et al.* (eds.), *New Bible Dictionary*. London: IVF.

——(1967), *The Epistle to the Romans. The English Text with Introduction, Exposition and Notes* 2. New London Commentary on the New Testament. 2nd edn. London and Edinburgh: Marshall, Morgan and Scott (1st edn 1965).

——(1977), *The Imputation of Adam's Sin*. Reissue. Nutley, NJ: Presbyterian and Reformed (1st edn 1959, and previously in articles in the *Westminster Theological Journal* 18–20).

Newman, John Henry (1893), *Apologia pro vitâ suâ, being a History of his Religious Opinions*. New edn. London: Longmans, Green and Co. (1st edn in book form 1865).

Nicole, Jules-Marcel (1986), *Le Livre de Job* 1. Commentaire Evangélique de la Bible. Vaux-sur-Seine: Edifac.

Niebuhr, Reinhold (1941), *The Nature and Destiny of Man. A Christian Interpretation*. 1: *Human Nature*. New York: Scribner's.

North, Gary (1968), *Marx's Religion of Revolution. The Doctrine of Creative Destruction*. Nutley, NJ: Craig Press.

O'Brien, Peter T. (1994), 'Divine Analysis and Comprehensive Solution: Some Priorities from Ephesians 2', *Reformed Theological Review* 53, 130–142.

O'Donovan, Oliver (1994). *Resurrection and Moral Order. An Outline for Evangelical Ethics*. 2nd edn. Leicester: Apollos. Grand Rapids: Eerdmans.

Pannenberg, Wolfhart (1994), *Systematic Theology* 2, trans. Geoffrey W. Bromiley. Grand Rapids: Eerdmans (German original 1991).

Papaïoannou, Kostas (1972), *Marx et les marxistes*. New revised edn. Paris: Flammarion (1st edn 1965).

Pascal, Blaise (1962), *Pascal's Pensées*, trans. Marvin Turnell. London: Harville.

Payne, J. Barton (1962), *The Theology of the Older Testament*. Grand Rapids: Zondervan.

Peters, Ted (1994), *Sin. Radical Evil in Soul and Society*. Grand Rapids: Eerdmans.

Pipkin, H. Wayne, and John H. Yoder (1989), trans. and ed.,

Balthasar Hubmaier. Theologian of Anabaptism. Classics of the Radical Reformation 5. Scottdale, Pa.: Herald.

Porter, J. R. (1965), 'The Legal Aspects of the Concept of "Corporate Personality" in the Old Testament', *Vetus Testamentum* 15, 361–380.

Porter, Stanley E. (1990a), 'The Pauline Concept of Original Sin, in Light of Rabbinical Background', *Tyndale Bulletin* 41/1, 3–30.

——(1990b), 'Two Myths: Corporate Personality and Language/Mentality Determinism', *Scottish Journal of Theology* 43, 289–307.

Rad, Gerhard von (1963), *Genesis: A Commentary*, trans. J. H. Marks. 2nd edn. London: SCM.

Ramm, Bernard (1985), *Offense to Reason.* San Francisco: Harper and Row.

Ricœur, Paul (1964), *Histoire et vérité.* 2nd edn. Paris: Seuil (1st edn 1955).

——(1967), *The Symbolism of Evil,* trans. Emerson Buchanan. Boston: Beacon (French original 1960).

——(1974a), 'Guilt, Ethics and Religion', trans. Charles Freilich, in P. Ricœur, *The Conflict of Interpretations. Essays in Hermeneutics,* ed. Don Ihde. Evanston: Northwestern University Press (French original of the book 1970).

——(1974b), 'The Hermeneutics of Symbols and Philosophical Reflection I', trans. Denis Savage, in P. Ricœur, *The Conflict of Interpretation. Essays in Hermeneutics,* ed. Don Ihde. Evanston: Northwestern University Press (French original of the book 1970).

——(1974c), 'Original Sin: A Study in Meaning', trans. Peter McCormick, in P. Ricœur, *The Conflict of Interpretations. Essays in Hermeneutics,* ed. Don Ihde. Evanston: Northwestern University Press (French original of the book 1970).

Rist, John M. (1994), *Augustine. Ancient Thought Baptized.* Cambridge: Cambridge University Press.

Robertson, O. Palmer (1980), *The Christ of the Covenants.* Grand Rapids: Baker.

Rogerson, J. W. (1970), 'The Hebrew Conception of "Corporate Personality": A Re-examination', *Journal of Theological Studies* 21, 1–16.

Romérowski, Sylvain (1995), 'L'opposition entre la chair et l'Esprit en Galates 5.17', *Fac-Réflexion* [Faculté Libre de

Théologie Evangélique, Vaux-sur-Seine] 33, 14–22.

Rondet, Henri (1967), *Le Péché originel dans la tradition patristique et théologique.* Paris: Fayard.

Ruffié, Jacques (1983), *De la biologie à la culture,* coll. Champs. Paris: Flammerion.

Rule, Andrew K. (1955), 'Time', in Lefferts A. Loetscher (ed.), *Twentieth Century Encyclopedia of Religious Knowledge* 2. Grand Rapids: Baker.

Scharbert, Josef (1968), *Prolegomena eines Alttestamentlers zur Erbsündenlehre.* Questiones disputatae 37. Freiburg–Basel–Vienna: Herder.

Schönborn, Christoph (1991a), Vorwort, in Ch. Schönborn *et al.*, *Zur kirchlichen Erbsündenlehre. Stellungnahmen zu einer brennenden Frage,* 7–10. Einsiedeln, Freiburg: Johannes Verlag.

——(1991b), 'Die kirchliche Erbsündenlehre im Umriss', in Ch. Schönborn *et al.*, *Zur kirchlichen Erbsündenlehre. Stellungnahmen zu einer brennenden Frage,* 69–102. Einsiedeln, Freiburg: Johannes Verlag.

Simeons, A. T. W. (1969), *La Psychosomatique, médecine de demain. La lutte contre les 'maladies de civilisation',* trans. Th. Henrot. Marabout Université. Verviers: Gérard et Cie (English original *Man's Presumptuous Brain.* London: Longmans, Green and Co., 1960).

Skinner, B. F. (1980), *Beyond Freedom and Dignity.* Toronto, *etc.*: Bantam (1st edn 1971).

Smith, David L. (1994), *With Willful Intent. A Theology of Sin.* Wheaton: Bridgepoint (= Victor Books).

Spaemann, R. (1991), 'Über einige Schwierigkeiten mit der Erbsündenlehre', in Ch. Schönborn *et al.*, *Zur kirchlichen Erbsündenlehre. Stellungnahmen zu einer brennenden Frage,* 39–66. Einsiedeln, Freiburg: Johannes Verlag.

Strimple, Robert B. (1987), 'Bernard Ramm and the Theology of Sin' [review of Ramm 1985], *Westminster Theological Journal* 49, 143–152.

Strong, Augustus H. (1907), *Systematic Theology.* Philadelphia: Judson.

Suchocki, Marjorie H. (1994), *The Fall to Violence. Original Sin in Relational Theology.* New York: Continuum.

Teilhard de Chardin, Pierre (1955), *Le Phénomène humain.* Oeuvres 1. Paris: Seuil.

——(1962), *La Place de l'homme dans la nature.* 10/18. Paris:

Union Générale d'Editions.

Théry, René (1975), 'La Responsabilité collective', in Paul Guilluy (ed.), *La Culpabilité fondamentale. Péché originel et anthropologie moderne*, 130–152. Gembloux: J. Duculot. Lille: Centre interdisciplinaire des Facultés catholiques.

Thibon, Gustave (1942), *Diagnostics. Essai de physiologie sociale*. Paris: Librairie de Médicis.

Tidiman, Brian (1987), *Le Livre d'Ezéchiel* 2. Commentaire Evangélique de la Bible. Vaux-sur-Seine: Edifac.

Todorov, Tzvetan (1992), *Au nom du peuple. Témoignages sur les camps communistes*, trans. from Bulgarian by Marie Vrinat. La Tour d'Aigues, France: Aube.

Tresmontant, Claude (1956), *Introduction à la pensée de Teilhard de Chardin*. Paris: Seuil.

Turretinus [Turretin], Franciscus [François] (1847), *Institutio theologiae elencticae* 1. New York: Robert Carter (first published 1679).

Twelftree, Graham H. (1992), 'Temptation of Jesus', in Joel B. Green, Scot McKnight and I. Howard Marshall (eds.), *Dictionary of Jesus and the Gospels*, 820a–827b. Leicester and Downers Grove, Ill.: IVP.

Vanneste, A. (1994), 'Le péché originel: un débat sans issue?' *Ephemerides Theologicae Lovanienses* 70, 359–383.

Van Til, Cornelius (1972), *Common Grace and the Gospel*. Nutley, NJ: Presbyterian and Reformed.

Viallaneix, Nelly (1979), *Ecoute Kierkegaard. Essai sur la communication de la Parole* 2. Cogitatio fidei 95. Paris: Cerf.

Wagner, C. Peter, and F. Douglas Pennoyer (eds.) (1990), *Wrestling with Dark Angels. Toward a Deeper Understanding of the Supernatural Forces in Spiritual Warfare*. Ventura, Ca: Regal.

Warfield, Benjamin B. (1970a), 'Hosea VI.7: Adam or Man?', in John E. Meeter (ed.), *Selected Shorter Writings of Benjamin B. Warfield*, 116–129. Nutley, NJ: Presbyterian and Reformed (article first published 1903, in *The Bible Student* 8, 1–10).

——(1970b), 'Repentance and Original Sin', in John E. Meeter (ed.), *Selected Shorter Writings of Benjamin B. Warfield*, 278–282. Nutley, NJ: Presbyterian and Reformed (article first published 1899, in *Union Seminary Magazine* 10, 169–174).

Williams, Norman P. (1927), *The Ideas of the Fall and of Original Sin. A Historical and Critical Study*. London: Longmans, Green and Co.

Index of authors

Index of Scripture references

Index of references to apocryphal and other ancient sources

Index of subjects

Adam, 18, 31ff., 37ff., 57, 61, 63ff., 84, 96ff., 100f., 114ff., 127ff.

Anabaptists, 15

analogy of faith, 17, 42

Antichrist, 92

anxiety, 53, 57f., 60f., 100, 112, 128

atonement, 24, 133

Augustinian thought, 15, 19, 22, 31f., 38, 53, 57, 64, 70f., 105ff., 109, 111f., 123, 131

auxilium quo / sine quo non, 57

biology, 106, 122, 125, 129

birth and new birth, 27, 29

bondage, 23, 99ff., 130, 135

children, 21, 23f., 31, 76, 84, 95, 133f.

Christ, 18, 32, 47f., 54, 63, 66ff., 70f., 75, 78ff., 97f., 132ff.

church, 91, 133

concupiscence, 20, 24, 29, 51, 59, 113, 124

corporate personality, 64, 96f., 107, 116

corruption, 20ff., 28ff., 33f., 65ff., 73, 81, 91ff., 103, 109, 127f., 134f.

covenant, 43, 49, 72, 77f., 80, 114, 116f., 127, 130

creation, 12, 19, 44ff., 49, 56ff., 77, 108f., 112, 122, 130ff.

cynicism, 11, 88

Darwinism, 37

death, 21, 33f., 45f., 48f., 55, 65ff., 70ff., 77f., 80, 88, 110, 112, 133, 135

depravity, 31, 67, 117, 120f., 127, 129f.

deprivation, 92, 121, 127f., 130

determinism, 19, 94f.

devil, 11, 18, 33, 44, 47, 96, 102, 126f., 129

dualism, 58, 92f., 122

Eden, 31, 34, 37, 40f., 43f., 47, 49, 57, 71, 88, 116, 127

ethics, 98, 106, 124

Eve, 22, 32ff., 39, 42, 46, 48, 50ff., 54, 65, 112

evil, 11, 35, 55ff., 61f., 85, 87, 89ff., 108, 127; *see also* metaphysical evil

evolution, 37, 39f., 56, 90

fall, 46, 50, 52, 54, 56, 59ff., 66, 71, 73, 80, 86, 92, 101, 108, 112, 114, 117, 121, 125f., 128

fate, 19, 59, 61, 99, 101, 107

flesh, 19, 22, 26f., 30, 124, 126, 130, 132ff.

freedom, 11, 19f., 33, 50, 61, 88, 90f., 94f., 97, 99f., 102, 106, 108, 122, 129ff.

genetics, 31, 95, 111, 117, 125f.

Gentiles, 26, 80

Gnosticism, 64

grace (common), 89

guilt, 11, 19, 23ff., 28, 31, 59, 70, 73, 75, 81, 84, 99f., 102, 106f., 111, 115, 119, 121, 123, 128ff., 134